Inhaltsverzeichnis

VORKURS **A**

Come and meet them

1

THE VERB *TO BE*

Write the short form, the negative and the question.

		SHORT FORM	NEGATIVE	QUESTION	
1	I am	______	______	–	
2	You are	______	______	______	
3	He is	______	______	______	
4	She is	______	______	______	from Europe
5	It is	______	______	______	
6	We are	______	______	______	
7	They are	______	______	______	

2

SHORT FORMS

Complete these sentences about Bart Simpson and his family. Use short forms where possible.

1 Hi! ______ Bart Simpson. W______ y______ name?

2 This ______ Lisa. S______ m______ sister.

3 T______ ______ m______ father, Homer. H______ a donuts fan.

4 No, Marge ______ m______ sister! S______ m______ mother.

5 M______ parents ______ from Germany. T______ from the USA.

6 W______ ______ a very big family, or very rich. W______ just a normal family.

7 This ______ o______ house. I______ ______ in Munich. I______ in Springfield, in the USA.

8 A______ y______ a Simpsons fan?

PRONOUNS

3 **Look at the pictures and complete Tom's statements with *my*, *your*, *his*, *her*, *our* or *their*.**

1 This is ___________ favourite rock group, the Rockos.

2 This is ___________ newest CD.

3 It isn't ___________ sweatshirt. It's ___________ sweatshirt.

4 This is ________ new discman.

5 What's ________ favourite rock group?

GENITIVE 'S

4 **Correct the sentences using 's.**

▶ **EXAMPLE** The discman of Tom is new. *Tom's discman is new.*

1 The sweatshirt of the girl is too big. The girl's sweatshirt is too big

2 The girl is the sister of Tom. The girl is Tom's sister

3 Tom wants to buy the new CD of the group. Tom wants to buy the group's new CD.

4 The name of Tom is on his sweatshirt. Tom's name is on his sweatshirt.

QUESTIONS

5 **Write the questions for these answers.**

1 ______________________________? – I'm 16 years old.

2 ______________________________? – My hobbies are surfing and hiphop.

3 ______________________________? – My birthday is in September.

4 ______________________________? – Bart Simpson? He's Joey's favourite Simpsons character.

5 ______________________________? – He's from the United States.

VORKURS B

What are you doing?

1

PRESENT CONTINUOUS

These people are all busy just now. Complete these sentences with the *-ing* form of a verb from the box.

play • plan • watch • listen to • write

▶ EXAMPLE Sharon and her friend *are planning* a party.

1 Greg is writing an email to Yasmin.

2 Sharon and her mum are watching the Simpsons on TV.

3 Joey and his brother are playing football.

4 Tom is eisting to his new Rockos CD.

2

PRESENT CONTINUOUS

Write each sentence from exercise 1 in the negative and as a question.

▶ EXAMPLE *Sharon and her friend aren't planning a party.*
Are Sharon and her friend planning a party?

1 ______________________________.

______________________________?

2 ______________________________.

______________________________?

3 ______________________________.

______________________________?

4 ______________________________.

______________________________?

3

TIMES

Write these times digitally.

▶ EXAMPLE quarter past nine *9.15*

1 8 o'clock ________

2 half past two ________

3 quarter to seven ________

4 half past three ________

5 twenty-five to eleven ________

Now look at the information and match a time to a question.

FC Bayern vs. Manchester United
Olympic stadium Munich
11 November 2005 7.30

Amsterdam – Cologne
Mon – Fri

Dep	*Arr*
08.35	18.15
10.35	20.15
12.35	22.45

English Conversation – Beginners:
Sat 9.15, room 204

New York Istanbul Sydney

Odeon Cinema
Aliens: 11.30, 14.30, 17.15

What: Surprise welcome-home party
Who for: Thelma
Where: 237 Elm Street
When: Sat 26 June, 8 p.m.

▶ **EXAMPLE** When is the English class? *It's at 9.15.*

a It's now 12 noon. When's the next film? It's at 2.30pm.
b What time is the party? It's at 8.00pm.
c What time is the football game? It's at 7.30p.m
d It's now half past nine. When's the next bus to Cologne? It's at 10.35a.m
e What time is it now in Sydney? It's at 11.45a.m

4 PRONOUNS

Unscramble the messages and complete each one with the correct form of a pronoun for the underlined word.

▶ **EXAMPLE** Sharon / visit / planning / is / to / Cologne *Sharon is planning to visit Cologne.*
Please call *her*.

1 We / a problem / our / have / computer/ with We have our a problem with computer
Can you help us ?

2 Greg / your parents / to meet / wants Greg wants to meet your parents.
Can you call him ?

3 I / at home / 'm / working I'm working at home .
Can you call me ?

4 They / your / new DVD / to watch / want They want you to watch new DVD.
Can you call them ?

VORKURS **C**

Can you tell me the way?

1 VOCABULARY

Fill in the gaps with words from Vorkurs C.

1 The ________________ is where you go to watch films.

2 I go to the ________________ ________________ to play football.

3 My dad goes to the ________________ to drink with his friends.

4 We go to the ________________ to get our money.

2 PREPOSITIONS

Look at the pictures and complete the sentences with the correct prepositions from the box.

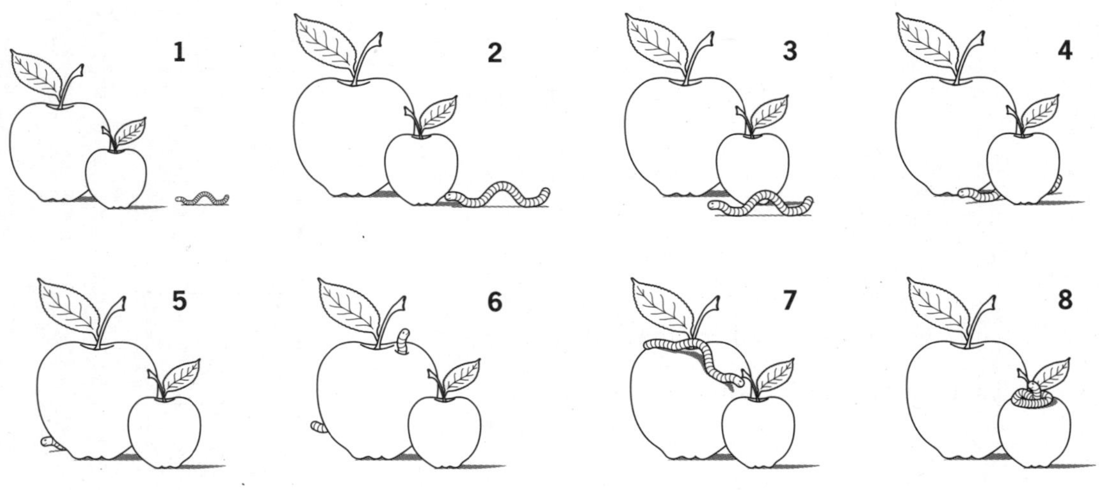

behind • between • in • in front of • ~~near~~ • next to • opposite • to

Where is the worm (= *Wurm*)?

1 It's *near*________________ the apples.

2 It's ________________ the small apple.

3 It's ________________ the small apple.

4 It's ________________ the apples.

5 It's ________________ the big apple.

6 It's ________________ the big apple.

7 It's going from the big apple ________________ the small apple.

8 The worm is ________________ you, and it's smiling at you.

3

THERE IS/ARE

What can you find in this new shopping centre? Look at this plan and complete the sentences with *There's a*, *There isn't a*, *There are (two)* or *There aren't any*.

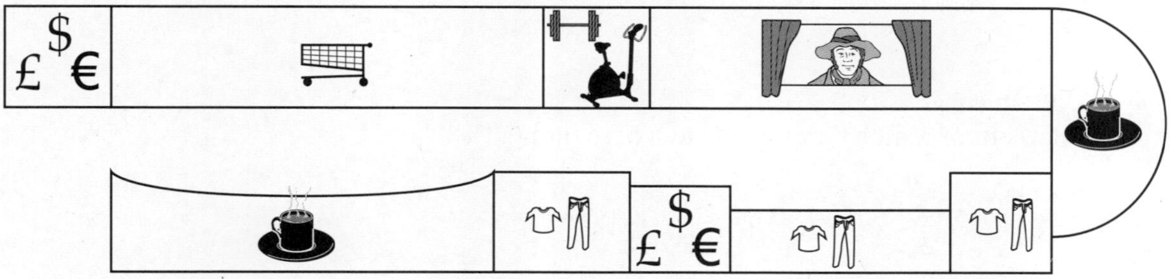

What is there in the shopping centre?

▶ EXAMPLE *There's a* supermarket. *There isn't a* swimming pool.

1 ______________________ fitness centre.

2 ______________________ discos.

3 ______________________ cinema.

4 ______________________ banks.

5 ______________________ cafés.

6 ______________________ school.

7 ______________________ boutiques.

8 ______________________ book shops.

4

QUESTIONS

What is the question?

1 Can ____________________________ Sharon, please?

– Speaking.

2 What ____________________________ next Saturday evening?

– I'm singing with my rap group at a club near here.

3 Can you ____________________________ to the club?

– Go along Pembroke Road, turn left into Kensington Park Road, and the club is number 74, near the bus stop.

4 Sorry. Can you ____________________________ ?

– Yes. Go along Pembroke Road, turn left into Kensington Park Road, and the club …

5 Pembroke ? How do you ____________________________ ?

– P-E-M-B-R-O-K-E

5

PLURAL OF NOUNS

Write the plural form of these nouns.

1 hobby ______________

2 file ______________

3 rapper ______________

4 message ______________

5 bus ______________

6 family ______________

7 church ______________

8 box ______________

TIP *In der Regel bildet man den Plural durch Anhängen von -s. Nomen, deren Endung im Singular Konsonant + -y ist, enden aber im Plural mit -ies (statt -y). An Nomen, die mit -s, -x, -ch enden, wird im Plural -es angehängt.*

VORKURS D I fancy her

VOCABULARY

1 How often? Match these words to a percentage (%).

manchmal nie oft normal immer
sometimes • never • often • usually • ~~always~~

100 % of the time	always	ca 30–69 % of the time	sometimes
ca 90–99 % of the time	often	0 % of the time	never
ca 70–89 % of the time	usualley		

SIMPLE PRESENT

2 Look at the pictures of different free time activities and write sentences about how often (*always, often, sometimes, never*) you do these things, and when (*in winter, in summer, in January, in August, at the weekend*, etc.).

▶ **EXAMPLE** *I never go swimming in winter.*

1 I often go sking in January.

2 I sometimes dancing to the music at the weekend.

3 He always playing football

4 ______________________

TRANSLATION

3 Complete the translation of these sentences about what the netpals do. Be careful with the sentence order!

TIP Adverbien der Häufigkeit werden vor das Vollverb des Satzes gestellt. Zeitangaben stehen am Anfang oder am Ende des Satzes.

1 Joey fährt immer im Januar Ski in Colorado.
In Colorado Joey ______________________ ______________________ in January.

2 In Australien verbringt Greg oft im Januar Nachmittage am Strand.
In Australia Greg ______________________ in January.

3 Sharon und ihre Rapgruppe singen meistens am Wochenende.
Sharon and ______________________ at the ______________.

4 Heike geht nie surfen.

Heike ____.

5 Greg hat oft Grillpartys im Dezember.

Greg ____.

6 Sharon geht manchmal am Wochenende auf Flohmärkte.

Sharon ______________________________ at the ______________.

4

LINKING WORDS

This is an email from Joey's friend in Munich. Complete the email with *and, because, but, so* or *then*.

Hi Joey!

How are you there in beautiful Colorado? Summer must be wonderful there. Sometimes it is here too, ___but___ [1] it isn't today. Usually I meet my friends in a beer garden on Friday afternoon. ___But___ [2] we can't go today ___because___ [3] it's raining a lot. ___So___ [4] we're going to a café at 6 o'clock ___and___ [5] ___then___ [6] we're going to the cinema. That's good for a rainy evening!!

1 selected

5

VOCABULARY

Complete this crossword.

1 Your brothers, sisters and parents are part of your … .
2 It's what you do in your freetime.
3 This is when you cook and eat food outside.
4 If your aunt and uncle have a son, he's your … .
5 You do it 99% of the time. You … do it.
6 His first name is Joey, and his family name or … is Chang.
7 You usually write and send this message on the computer.
8 In Europe and the USA it's time for swimming and beach parties.
9 This festival in Europe usually ends in February.
10 Saturday and Sunday.

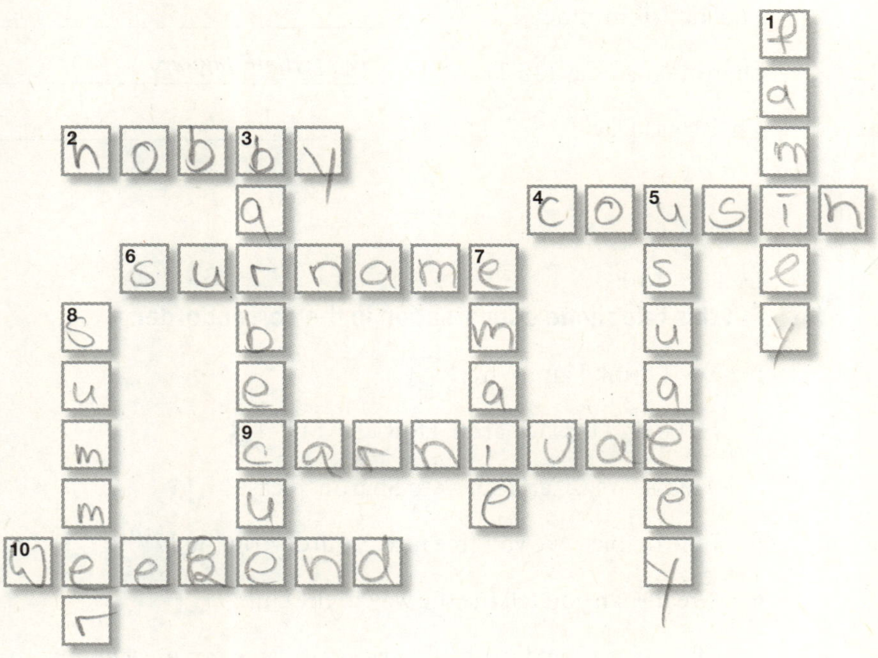

VORKURS E

It's me, Greg

1 VOCABULARY: DAYS OF THE WEEK

Complete the puzzle *(= Rätsel)*.

1 This is the first day of the weekend.
2 This is the first day of the school week.
3 This is the last day before the weekend.
4 This is the day in the middle of the week.
5 This is the day when many people go to church and the shops aren't open.
6 This is the fourth day of the week.

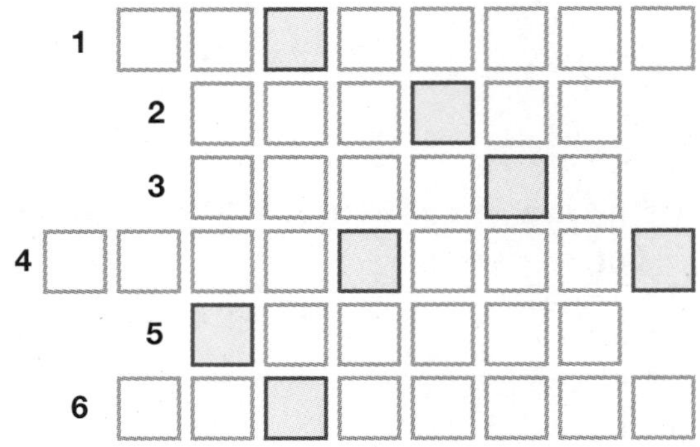

The letters in the grey boxes make another day of the week: ______________________

2 DATES

Write out these dates and put them in order.

Valentine's Day	______________________	☐
Joey's birthday (26.4)	______________________	☐
New Year's Eve (= *Silvester*)	______________________	☐
Heike's birthday (3.6)	______________________	☐
First day of summer	______________________	☐
Sharon's birthday (15.1)	the 15th of January	1
Christmas Day	______________________	☐

3 TELEPHONING

Put this telephone conversation in the correct order.

a Yes, I think I am. Why? ☐
b Hi Greg. This is Sharon. How are you? ☐
c This is Greg. Can I speak to Sharon, please? 1
d Fine thanks. Are you free next Saturday, on the 17th? ☐
e Great! Can you tell me the way to the club? ☐
f Oh, sorry, I don't really like cricket. But we can meet at my rap group club in the evening. ☐
g Well, I have tickets for a cricket game at 2.30. Do you want to go? ☐

4 THE VERB *TO LIKE*

Look at the table. (✔= They like these things. ✘ = They don't like these things.)
Complete the sentences about the five netpals with the correct form of *like*.

	cricket	beach parties	carnival	skiing	flea markets	ice cream
Joey	✘	✔	✘	✔	✔	✘
Greg	✔	✔	✘	✔	✔	✘
Heike	✔	✘	✔	✘	✔	✘
Sharon	✘	✔	✘	✔	✘	✔
Yasmin	✘	✔	✘	✔	✘	✔

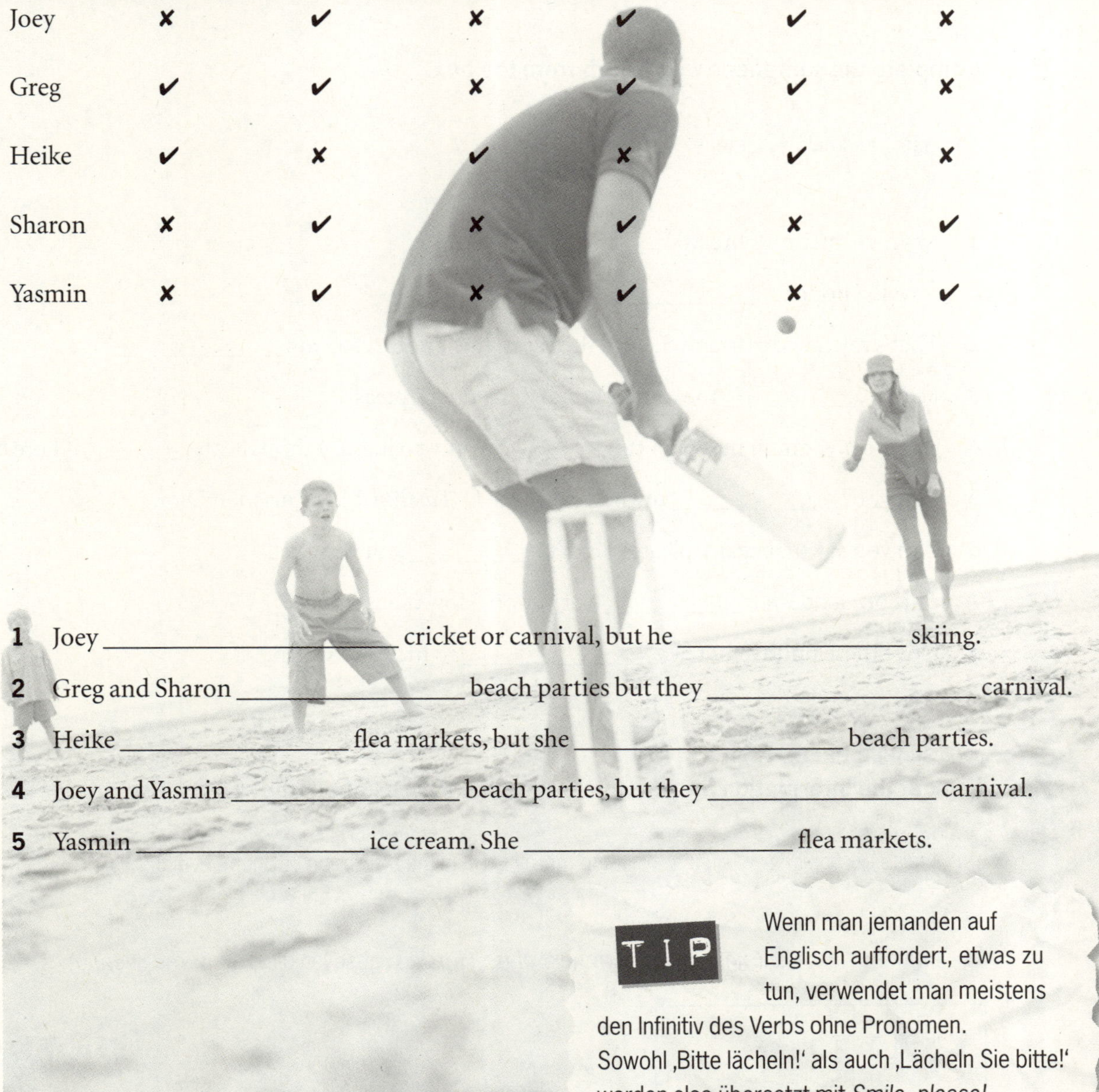

1 Joey ______________________ cricket or carnival, but he _________________ skiing.
2 Greg and Sharon _________________ beach parties but they ____________________ carnival.
3 Heike _________________ flea markets, but she ____________________ beach parties.
4 Joey and Yasmin _________________ beach parties, but they _________________ carnival.
5 Yasmin _________________ ice cream. She ____________________ flea markets.

TIP Wenn man jemanden auf Englisch auffordert, etwas zu tun, verwendet man meistens den Infinitiv des Verbs ohne Pronomen. Sowohl ‚Bitte lächeln!' als auch ‚Lächeln Sie bitte!' werden also übersetzt mit *Smile, please!*

5 TRANSLATION: COMMANDS

Translate these sentences into English.

a Ruf mich bitte heute abend nicht an. ____
b Erzählen Sie mir von John. ____
c Hier parken. ____
d Ruf mich zurück! ____
e Sagen Sie es bitte noch mal. ____
f Warten Sie nicht auf mich. ____
g Geh nach Hause. ____

▶▶▶

UNIT 1 The colour of music

1 VOCABULARY

Complete the sentences with a verb from the box.

hear • smell • taste • see • feel

1 M-m-m-m! Fresh bread! It ____________ fantastic!

– Well, I hope it ______________ good, too.

2 That's my new girlfriend behind the car in this photo. Can you _____________ her?

3 I can't ____________ the music. Louder (= *lauter*), please.

4 There's no light in here, so I can't __________ my coat. But I think I can _________ it here on the sofa.

5 Can you ______________ my new perfume (= *Parfüm*)? It's Christian Dior.

6 Can you say that again, please? I can't ___________ you very well.

7 This pizza doesn't ____________ very good. How old is it?

8 I love these pullovers. They _______________ so nice and warm.

2 THE SIMPLE PRESENT

Look at the information and complete these sentences about the events. Use the words in the box.

starts • finishes • meets • in the morning • in the afternoon • in the evening

▶ **EXAMPLE** *The English for Beginners class finishes* at seven o'clock *in the evening.*

SEP 1
Annual Flea Market,
Newbury. On the Common.
9:30am–4pm. 802-866-5580

Fit For Fun
Rollerdisco
(11:00–18:30 Family and Birthday-Skating)

7:45 Ali
(R, '01)
*** With
Will Smith.

English for Beginners
Mondays and
Wednesdays,
5:30–7:00.
Tel. 704-415-9735

RAP CLUB –
for all age groups
7:30, Thursday,
51 Crescent Gardens, Reading

Blue Monday Band
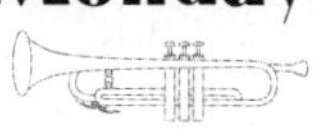
Every Monday from 8.30
at Stoney Teen Centre

1 ______________________________ at four o'clock ______________________.

2 ______________________________ at half past six ______________________.

3 ______________________________ at quarter to eight ______________________.

4 ____ at half past five ______________.

5 ______________________________ at half past eight ______________________.

6 ______________________________ at half past seven ______________________.

7 ______________________________ at eleven o'clock ______________________.

8 ______________________________ at half past nine ______________________.

Use the same information to complete these questions with the words in the box.

do/does • start • finish • meet

▶ **EXAMPLE** When *does* the film Ali *start*? At 3.45

a When ____________ the English class ____________? At 7.00

b What time ____________ the rollerdisco ____________? At 11.00

c What time ____________ the rollerdisco ____________? At 6.30

d When ____________ the flea market ____________? At 9.30

e What time ____________ the flea market ____________? At 4.00

f What time ____________ the members of the rap club ____________? At 7.30

g When ____________ the band ____________? At 8.30

h When ____________ the English classes ____________? At 5.30

3

THE SIMPLE PRESENT

Toby Gates is a soap opera actor and works with Ray Trekker at the studio. Complete each part of the text about his daily routine with the correct verb from the box.

thinks • stay • gets up • leaves • enjoys • start • speak • starts • goes • like • go • meets • plays • finishes • has • ask

Soap opera actors usually __________ [1] work very early, so from Monday to Friday Toby __________ [2] at 5.30, and __________ [3] the house at about 6.30. He __________ [4] work at 7.00 and __________ [5] at about 5 in the afternoon. It's a very long day. But Toby really __________ [6] his job. A lot of fans __________ [7] to him on the street and __________ [8] him for his autograph (= *Autogramm*). He usually __________ [9] that's fun. Because he __________ [10] such a long day at the studio, he usually __________ [11] to bed early from Sunday to Thursday. Toby and his girlfriend really __________ [12] Ray Trekker and his live disco, so on Friday they sometimes __________ [13] there. They __________ [14] until 1 or 2 o'clock in the morning. On Saturday and Sunday he often __________ [15] friends and __________ [16] football with his club.

4

THE SIMPLE PRESENT

A German exchange student, Silke, gets the chance to interview Toby Gates for her school newspaper. Put the words in the correct order for her questions. Then use the information above to complete Toby's answers.

Silke's questions	Toby's answers
1 get up / When / you / do / usually ______________________________	At __________.
2 you / at the weekend / get up / Do /so early / too ______________________________	No, I __________.
3 drive / you / studio / to the / Do ______________________________	No, I __________. I go by bike.
4 work / Ray Trekker / Does / in your studio / too ______________________________	Yes, he __________.
5 do / you and the other actors / start work / When ______________________________	At __________.
6 often / you / go out / in the evening / Do ______________________________	No, I __________.
7 you / your fans / sometimes / Do / meet ______________________________	Yes, I __________.
8 they / your autograph / Do / ask for ______________________________	Yes, they __________.

Write two more questions that you would like to ask Toby.

____

____

5

THE SIMPLE PRESENT – NEGATIVES

Write negative sentences.

EXAMPLE Tony *doesn't work* (not / work) with Ray.
Toby and the other actors *don't work* (not / work) at the weekend.

1 Toby ____________ (not / stay) in bed late Monday to Friday.

2 The soap opera actors ____________ (not / finish) work early.

3 Toby ____________ (not / get up) early on Sunday.

4 Toby's girlfriend ____________ (not / like) the soap opera.

5 Toby and his girlfriend ____________ (not / go) to the disco on Monday.

6 Toby's fans ____________ (not / call) him at home.

7 Toby and Ray ____________ (not / work) for a radio studio.

8 Toby ____________ (not / meet) the other actors at the weekend.

6

EVERYDAY ENGLISH: MEETING PEOPLE

Put the dialogue in the correct order.

a Yes, I do. It's really great! Oh, sorry! That's my mobile phone. ☐

b That's OK. Ray wants some help with the next song. See you later. ☐

c I feel great! It's Friday! This is my girlfriend, Gloria Cooper.
Gloria, Silke is an exchange student here. ☐

d Fine thanks, Toby. And how are you? ☐

e OK, goodbye. ☐

f Hi, Silke! This is a great disco, isn't it? How are you? 1

g Nice to meet you, Silke. Do you like this band's music? ☐

UNIT 2
Fitness

1
SIMPLE PRESENT OR PRESENT CONTINUOUS?

Complete the sentences with the verbs in brackets in the simple present or present continuous.

EXAMPLE Jacko *usually meets* (usually meet) friends at the weekend in winter, but this weekend he *is working* (work) in his uncle's bistro.

1 Jacko ______________ (not / usually watch) TV in the morning, but today there's no school or work, so he ______________ (watch) the Simpsons.

2 Jacko ______________ (often visit) his grandparents on Christmas Day, but this Christmas he and his family ______________ (go) to a restaurant for dinner.

3 Heike, Jacko's German friend, ______________ (usually celebrate) Carnival in Cologne, but this year she ______________ (celebrate) in Venice.

4 Jacko and Tracy ______________ (not / usually eat) fast food, but today is their brother's birthday, so they ______________ (have) lunch at Mc Donald's.

5 Jacko and his friends usually ______________ (sing) at their rap club on Saturday, but it's closed for the holidays so they ______________ (not / sing) there this evening.

2
SIMPLE PRESENT OR PRESENT CONTINUOUS?

What do they usually do? What are they doing now? Use the words to write questions.

EXAMPLE you / usually / go shopping / Saturday morning? *Do you usually go shopping on Saturday morning?*
you / go shopping / this Saturday? *Are you going shopping this Saturday?*

1 on Saturday / Wayne and Tracy / usually / surf / at the beach?

____

they / surf / at the beach / today?

____

2 Jacko / usually / check / his email at 4 o'clock?

____

he / check / his email / now?

____

3 Tracy / usually / listen to / hiphop?

____

she / listen to / hiphop / now?

____

4 Ronnie Campbell / play football / every day?

____

she / play football / today?

____

5 Jacko's parents / often / eat / fast food?

____

they / eat / fast food / for lunch today?

____

PRESENT CONTINUOUS

3 Sports-4-U is a big sports company. Next Monday a women's football team is coming to discuss a sponsorship deal *(= Sponsorenvertrag)* with Sports-4-U. Look at the plan for Monday and say what the trainees are doing.

▶ **EXAMPLE** Cindy *is working* at reception from 8 o'clock to 12 o'clock.

At 8 o'clock Dick ____________________ the T-shirts from Magic Print.

From 8.00 to 11.00 Julie and Greg ____________________ the conference room.

At 11 o'clock Julie and Greg ____________________ for the team.

Dick ____________________ at 11 o'clock.

Cindy, Greg and Dick ____________________ from 12.00 to 13.00 and Julie ____________________ then.

At 2 p.m. Greg and Julie ____________________ the team at the station.

At the same time, Dick ____________________ at reception, and Cindy ____________________ coffee and sandwiches for the team.

At 4 p.m. there's an interview with the team members and Cindy, Greg and Julie ____________________ a video of it.

Dick can't go to the interview because he ____________________ then.

At 7 p.m. everybody ____________________ to the Lighthouse Restaurant for dinner.

Trainee Jobs for Monday, 8 August

8.00	Cindy – work at reception Dick – pick up 150 Sports-4-U T-shirts from *Magic Print*, 227 North Street Julie, Greg – prepare conference room for interview
11.00	Julie, Greg – make photocopies for the team Dick – check video camera
12.00	Cindy, Greg, Dick – lunch Julie – work at reception
13.00	Julie – lunch Cindy – reception
14.00	Greg, Julie – meet the team members at the station Cindy – make coffee and sandwiches for the team Dick – work at reception
16.00	Cindy, Greg, Julie – make video of the interview with the team Dick – work at reception
19.00	Everybody – go to the Lighthouse Restaurant for dinner

4

EVERYDAY ENGLISH: TELLING SOMEONE THE WAY

Two of the team can't come to the interview at Sports 4-U, but they are in town and would like to meet the others for dinner at the Lighthouse Restaurant. Look at the map, and complete the email to them.

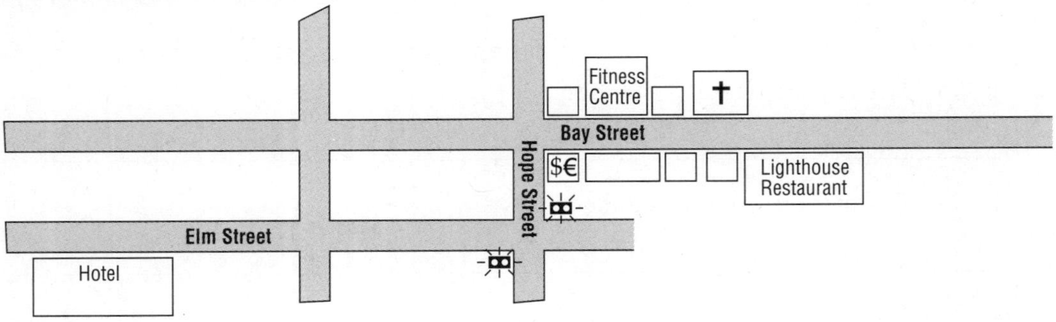

Dear Ms Howard and Ms White

It is so nice that you can meet us for dinner at the Lighthouse Restaurant.

You can easily walk there from your hotel. Here is how you get there. Leave your hotel and

t__________ r__________ 1. G__________ a__________ 2 Elm Street until you

c__________ 3 to the t__________ l__________ 4. It's the s__________ 5 street.

T__________ l__________ 6 into Hope Street and at the f__________ 7 street

t__________ r__________ 8 into Bay Street. Go p__________ 9 the bank, the fitness centre

and the church. The Lighthouse Restaurant is the f__________ b__________ 10 on the right.

5

PEOPLE AT WORK: DEPARTMENTS IN A BUILDING

This company has a lot of facilities (= *Anlagen*) for its employees and customers. Look at the plan, and say what there is and which floor it is on.

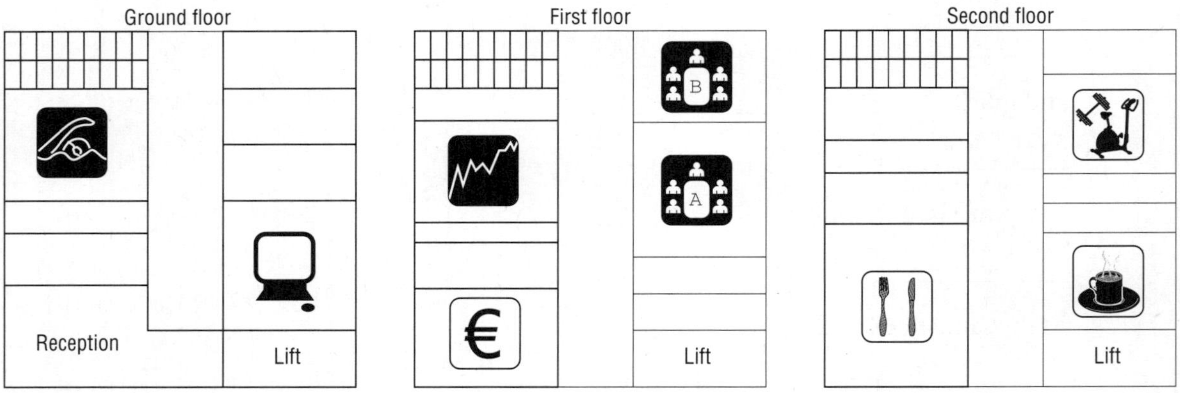

1 There's a ____________________ on the ____________________ floor.

2 T__________ two____________________ on the __________ floor.

3 T____.

4 T____.

6 EVERYDAY ENGLISH / PEOPLE AT WORK: HELPING A VISITOR

Complete these questions and answers at the reception desk.

1 Excuse me, where's ________________?

– It's on the ______________, just ______________ the lift.

2 Excuse me, where's ________________________?

– It's on the ______________, just ______________ finance.

3 Excuse me, where's ________________________?

– It's here on the __________________, over there ________ ________ ________.

4 Excuse me, where's the __________________?

– T________ the l________ to the __________________. It's __________ the lift and the fitness centre.

7 VOCABULARY: SPORTS

Answer the questions and fill in the words. What is the mystery word?

1 Can you … soccer or baseball?
2 If you want to be good at a sport, you must … a lot.
3 At a fitness centre or at home, these very active exercises are best with music.
4 In the USA they say soccer, but in England they say … .
5 After you do a lot of sport or work, you usually want to … for a short time.
6 Michael Jordan and Dirk Nowitzki are famous … players.
7 For baseball you need two … of nine players.
8 You do this in lakes and the sea in summer, or in a pool in winter.
9 You don't do any sport? What a … potato!
10 I like sports. I think they're lots of … .
11 Is that hockey team in a national … ?
12 9 or 18 holes, and Tiger Woods favourite game.

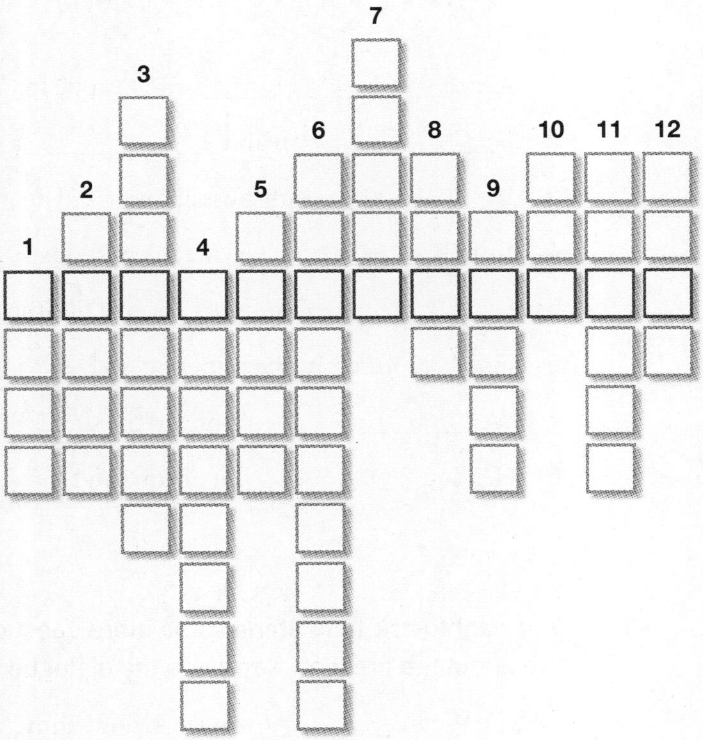

What is the opposite of the mystery word? ______________________________

UNIT 3

Jobs and stories

1

SIMPLE PAST – THE VERB *TO BE*

You're talking to Cathy O'Connor about her accident. Complete the dialogue with *was*, *were*, *wasn't* and *weren't*.

YOU Cathy, where ______________ [1] you when the accident happened?

CATHY I ____________ [2] on my way to work.

YOU _________________ [3] there a lot of workers on the building site?

CATHY No, there ________________ [4]. Only two or three.

YOU What about the poodle? _____________ [5] he dead?

CATHY No, he ______________ [6]. They took him to the vet (= *Tierarzt*) and now he's fine.

2

SIMPLE PAST

Shing Mei is telling her story again to some friends. Complete these sentences with a verb from the box in the simple past.

send • find • arrive • buy • die • fly • try • open • tell • give • phone

1 A box _________________ from Europe for a very famous singer.

2 I _______________ it and ______________ a dead dog.

3 I _______________ my boss about it and he ______________ the singer and asked her not to come.

4 Later he ______________ me to pet shops.

5 I _______________ to find a dog just like the one in the box.

6 Finally I found just the right dog, so I ________________ it.

7 We _______________ the box to the singer but she wasn't happy.

8 Her dog _____________ in Europe and she ___________ it back to Canada to bury it.

3

SIMPLE PRESENT OR SIMPLE PAST?

You want to ask Tony Stone some more questions. Some of these are about the past, and some are about the present. Complete the dialogue with *do*, *don't*, *did* and *didn't*.

YOU Where _________ [1] you work now, Tony?

TONY In a big hotel. Thank God, I _____________ [2] work in that terrible restaurant anymore.

YOU How long ___________ [3] you work there?

TONY About six weeks. I ________________ [4] like it very much.

YOU What happened to that customer who ate the beer mat? ___________ [5] he come back?

TONY No, he _____________ [6].

4 SIMPLE PAST

Fill in the simple past of the verbs in brackets. Then complete the sentences with a phrase from the box.

of a big company • in his hand • for nine months • as a mechanic • to a small room • for an interview

1 Tony Baxter_____________ (do) an apprenticeship _____________ _________________.

2 He ______________ (lose) his job and was unemployed _________ _________________.

3 His girlfriend ______________ (give) him the telephone number __________________________.

4 He _______________ (go) to the company ________________________.

5 The secretary ___________ (take) him _____________________________.

6 She ________________ (put) a 72-page questionnaire ____________________________.

5 TRANSLATION

Translate these sentences.

TIP ***Nicht vergessen!***

- *Ich habe ihn gestern gesehen = I saw him yesterday.* Die Zeitangabe steht am Anfang oder am Ende des Satzes.
- *vor drei Tagen = three days ago*

▶ **EXAMPLE** Wir haben letzten Samstag Fußball gespielt.
We played football last Saturday.

1 Er hat letzten Sommer seinen Job verloren.

____

2 Er ist gestern um 10 Uhr gegangen.

____

3 Sie hat vor fünf Jahren bei dieser Firma angefangen.

____

4 Hat er dich gestern angerufen?

____

5 Hat die Rapgruppe letzten Samstag in diesem Club gesungen?

____

6 Er hat letztes Jahr für Sports-4-U gearbeitet.

____

7 Hat seine Sekretärin auch dann für ihn gearbeitet?

____

8 Ich habe letzten Sommer zwei Wochen in den USA verbracht.

____

EVERYDAY ENGLISH: FILLING IN A FORM

6 **Coleg Powys is a vocational school *(Berufschule)* in Wales. Here is a form for students who would like more information about courses there. Complete the form with the information in the box.**

CF16 4HU • Johnny Thomas • 15 June 1985 • 337 Brentwood Road, Cardiff • johnnyt@hotmail.uk • p. 16 Computer Programming • (02920) 27648 • p. 27 Sport Leisure & Tourism

Enquiry Coleg Powys

Name ....

Address ....

....

....

Post Code ....

Tel ....

Your e-mail address ....

Date of Birth ....

Would like more information on the following courses

....

....

....

....

....

....

....

....

SIMPLE PAST / PEOPLE AT WORK

7 **Complete the sentences 1–6, and a–f with the simple past of the verb in brackets, then find the two sentences that go together.**

▶ EXAMPLE 1c
A bricklayer *worked* (work) here yesterday. – *Did he build* (he / build) this wall?

1 A bricklayer *worked* ______ (work) here yesterday. [c]

2 There ______ (be) two carpenters in our office yesterday. [ ]

3 The electrician finally ______ (come) this morning at 11 o'clock. [ ]

4 ______ (you / call) the plumber? [ ]

5 ______ (be) the foreman and the site manager good? [ ]

6 ______ (scaffolder / come) on time? [ ]

a ______ (she / repair) these lights?

b Yes, but he ______ (not / build) the scaffolding (= *Gerüst*) high enough.

c *Did he build* ______ (he / build) this wall?

d They ______ (finish) the tables.

e Of course, and he ______ (repair) the toilet very quickly.

f Well, they certainly ______ (tell) everybody what to do!

8 PEOPLE AT WORK: JOBS

Fill in the correct words about jobs in the spaces. The letters in the grey boxes from top to bottom give you a new word.

1 If you can't find a job for your sort of work, you will have to ... .
2 If you haven't got a job, you are ... .
3 That company is offering a good job, so you should make an ... with the personnel manager.
4 This person tells the builders what to do.
5 This person can install your lights.
6 This person makes tables and chairs.
7 Red, orange or blue? This person can change the colour of your room.
8 Before the house is finished, it's a ... site.
9 At a bank, the bank ... can help you change money and get cash.
10 People at work often eat here.
11 Nobody's perfect! It's easy to make a ... in any job.
12 This person fixes your car or motorbike.
13 This person builds walls.
14 This person fixes your toilet.

The mystery word: All of the people in the jobs above started with this.

UNIT 4

Clothes and shopping

COMPARISON OF ADJECTIVES

1 **Write the comparative and superlative forms of these adjectives.**

Adjective	Comparative	Superlative
funny	*funnier*	*the funniest*
attractive		
cheap		
expensive		
small		
big		
comfortable		
old		
new		
colourful		
fashionable		
warm		

COMPARISON OF ADJECTIVES

2 **Compare Jack's and Jill's clothes. Look at the pictures and use the words in the box on p. 25 in the correct form to write complete sentences.**

* Niemand außer mir ist vollkommen

big • ~~cheap~~ • colourful • comfortable • expensive • funny • small • warm

EXAMPLE It's €44. Jack's *pullover is cheaper than* Jill's.

1 It's blue, purple, beige and pink. Jill's ______________________________ Jack's.

2 They're size 38. Jill's ______________________________ Jack's.

3 They're size XL. Jack's ______________________________ Jill's.

4 Nobody is perfect but me. Jack's ______________________________ Jill's.

5 They're trainers, not high heels (= *hochhackige Schuhe*)! Jack's ______________________________ Jill's.

6 It's wool (= *Wolle*), not cotton (= *Baumwolle*). Jill's ______________________________ Jack's.

7 They're from a designer and cost €250. Jill's ______________________________ Jack's.

3 COMPARISON OF ADJECTIVES

Now look at Jerry's clothes and compare them with Jack's and Jill's. Look at the example and write more sentences.

EXAMPLE jeans / small *Jill has the smallest jeans.*

1 pullover / colourful ______________________________

2 T-shirt / funny ______________________________

3 jeans / expensive ______________________________

4 shoes / comfortable ______________________________

5 pullover / cheap ______________________________

6 pullover / expensive ______________________________

7 jeans / big ______________________________

4 RELATIVE CLAUSES + VOCABULARY

Fill in the gaps with *who* or *which* and then find the missing words in the puzzle below.

1 A person ____________ spends more money than he/she has, has d[e][b][t][s].

2 A b[ ][ ][ ][ ][ ][ ][ ] is a type of shop ____________ sells clothes.

3 A piece of plastic ____________ you can use like money is a c[ ][ ][ ][ ][ ] [ ][ ][ ][ ].

4 A c[ ][ ][ ][ ][ ][ ][ ][ ] is a book ____________ has lots of things you can buy in it.

5 A t[ ][ ][ ][ ][ ][ ][ ] is someone ____________ is between 13 and 19 years old.

6 T[ ][ ][ ][ ][ ][ ][ ] are shoes ____________ you wear to play sport in.

7 A j[ ][ ][ ][ ][ ] is something ____________ you put on to go outside.

8 S[ ][ ][ ][ ][ ] -hand shops sell clothes ____________ aren't new.

C	R	E	D	I	T	C	A	R	D
A	H	D	E	B	T	S	R	G	K
T	L	Q	U	J	I	U	D	J	T
A	E	A	T	A	I	F	V	S	R
L	N	S	E	C	O	N	D	H	A
O	M	P	E	K	Q	C	R	K	I
G	B	S	D	E	U	G	P	L	N
U	B	O	U	T	I	Q	U	E	E
E	A	F	N	C	O	M	W	O	R
T	E	E	N	A	G	E	R	B	S

5 RELATIVE CLAUSES

Match the parts to complete the sentences.

1 Sarah is somebody [d]

2 She's a model and always wears designer clothes [ ]

3 She travels to a lot of different places like Paris [ ]

4 Sarah works with many designers [ ]

5 Sarah's brother works in a boutique [ ]

6 He goes to all of Sarah's fashion shows [ ]

a which is a really exciting city.

b which always give him ideas for his boutique.

c which sells the latest clothes.

d who is happy with her job.

e which are normally too expensive for her to buy.

f who all try and make the coolest clothes.

6 PEOPLE AT WORK: SHOPPING DIALOGUES

Put the dialogues in the correct order.

1 Looking for tennis balls

- **a** Sorry, we haven't got them here. You have to go to the sport's department. ☐
- **b** Thank you very much. ☐
- **c** Where can I find that? ☐
- **d** Can I help you? [1]
- **e** You can take the lift to the fifth floor. ☐
- **f** Yes, I hope so. I'm looking for tennis balls. ☐

2 Buying a T-shirt

- **a** Yes, you can … Okay. That's £7 on your card. ☐
- **b** Good morning. I'd like to buy this T-shirt, please. [1]
- **c** That's £7 then, please. ☐
- **d** Would you like anything else? ☐
- **e** Can I pay with my credit card? ☐
- **f** No, thank you. ☐
- **g** Thank you. Bye. ☐

7 EVERYDAY ENGLISH / PEOPLE AT WORK: HELPING A CUSTOMER

The customer in the photo needs some help. Fill in the gaps in the dialogue with words from the box.

smaller • changing rooms • suits • cash desk •
big • colour • anything else • help • take • feel

SHOP ASSISTANT Good morning. Can I ____________________[1] you?

CUSTOMER Yes, please. Can I try these trousers and this T-shirt on, please?

SHOP ASSISTANT Yes, the ____________________[2] are this way.

CUSTOMER Thank you.

…

SHOP ASSISTANT How do they ____________________[3]?

CUSTOMER The trousers are a bit ____________________[4]. I need this belt to keep them on!

SHOP ASSISTANT I'll see if we have them in a size ____________________[5].

…

SHOP ASSISTANT Does that feel better?

CUSTOMER Yes, thank you.

SHOP ASSISTANT I think the T-shirt really ____________________[6] you.

Grey is a good ____________________[7] for you.

CUSTOMER Thank you. I'll ____________________[8] them.

SHOP ASSISTANT Would you like ____________________[9]?

CUSTOMER No, thank you. That's everything.

SHOP ASSISTANT Okay. The ____________________[10] is over there near the door.

CUSTOMER Thank you. Bye.

UNIT **5** # The USA, from east to west

1

SIMPLE PAST AND PRESENT PERFECT

Put the verbs in brackets into the simple past.

Sarah __________[1] (go) on holiday to New York last month. She __________[2] (visit) her friend Sally, who she __________[3] (meet) a couple of years ago in England. She __________[4] (fly) to the USA on Monday and on Tuesday she __________[5] (eat) dinner at a restaurant near Central Park with Sally. She __________[6] (come) back to England after a week of fun in New York!

Now finish the rest of the story using the present perfect.

Sarah ______________________________[7] (just write) a letter to Sally to say thank you for a lovely holiday. She ______________________________[8] (already start) to plan her next trip to America. She __________________________[9] (not drive) anywhere in the USA yet but she ____________________ __________________[10] (recently find) a travel company that sells driving holidays. She ____________ __________________[11] (never be) to Florida and so that's why she ___________________________[12] (book) to go there for her next holiday!

2

SIGNAL WORDS – SIMPLE PAST OR PRESENT PERFECT?

Fill in the gaps with the verbs in the simple past or present perfect.
Some of the signal words in bold print (*fett gedruckt*) are in Exercise 1.
Look at them to find out if they go with the simple past or the present perfect.

1 __________________________________ the Empire State Building **yet**? (you / visit)
2 I __________________________________ a lot of presents. (**already** / buy)
3 I _______________ a lot of shopping **yesterday**. (do)
4 I __________________________________ any photos **so far**. (not / take)
5 I _______________ in Los Angeles **last year**. (stay)
6 I__________________________________ in New York. (**just** / arrive)
7 I ______________ to Las Vegas **two years ago**. (fly)
8 I__________________________________ to the United States. (**never** / be)
9 We ______________ in a restaurant **last night**. (eat)
10 **When** __________________________________ Chicago? (you leave)

3 PRESENT PERFECT

Marty and Peggy are planning a party for Amy and Rory at their sports club in New York. Look at the checklists and complete the questions and answers with the present perfect.

Do for party – Marty

- Meet the DJ and plan the music ✓
- Give the DJ the keys for the club
- Check the plates and glasses ✓
- Buy drinks ✓
- Take drinks to club
- Clean party room ✓

Do for party – Peggy

- Send invitations by email ✓
- Make table decorations
- Drive to Tom's and get CDs ✓
- Make cakes ✓
- Buy bread and cheese and snacks ✓
- Take CDs and food to club

▶ **EXAMPLE** Marty *Have you sent* the invitations (*Einladungen*) yet?

Peggy Of course, I have.

	Marty	Peggy
1	______ the table decorations?	I ______ (start) them, but I ______ (not / finish) yet.
2	______ CDs from Tom?	Yes, I ______ .
3	______ cakes?	Yes, I ______ (do) that too.
4	______ food yet?	Yes, but I ______ (not / take) it to the club yet.

	Peggy	Marty
5	______ the DJ yet?	Yes, I ______ . But I ______ (not / give) him the keys for the club yet.
6	______ plates and glasses?	Yes, I ______ . They were dirty, as usual.
7	And ______ the drinks?	Yes, I ______ .
8	______ them to the club?	No, sorry. I ______ (not / have) time.
9	______ the party room?	Yes, I ______ (just / clean) it. It was really dirty!

4

SIMPLE PAST OR PRESENT PERFECT?

Here is a postcard that Amy sent to her sister who lives in England. Complete it with the simple past or present perfect of the verbs in brackets.

Hi!

We ________________ 1 (just arrive) in Denver and so far we ________________ 2 (cross) eight states and ________________ 3 (drive) almost 3000 miles. We ________________ 4 (spend) three nights in the car so far, but this morning I really ________________ 5 (start) to feel stiff, so a few hours ago we ________________ 6 (find) a nice and inexpensive motel for the night. So far we ________________ 7 (have) a great trip. We ________________ 8 (meet) some interesting people. Last Wednesday, in Ft. Wayne, Indiana, a very nice family ________________ 9 (invite) us to stay with them.

There ________________ 10 (be) some problems with the car recently. In Chicago last Friday we ________________ 11 (have) a breakdown, but a very nice mechanic ________________ 12 (repair) the car and it ________________ 13 (not / cost) too much money.

________________ 14 (you / hear) from Marty yet? She wanted to send you pictures of the party in New York. Hope you like them!

I have to go. Rory ________________ 15 (just come) in from a walk, and he wants to go get something to eat.

I'll send you another postcard when we get to California.

love,

Amy

5

VOCABULARY: TRAFFIC IN THE USA

Complete the crossword with words from unit 5.

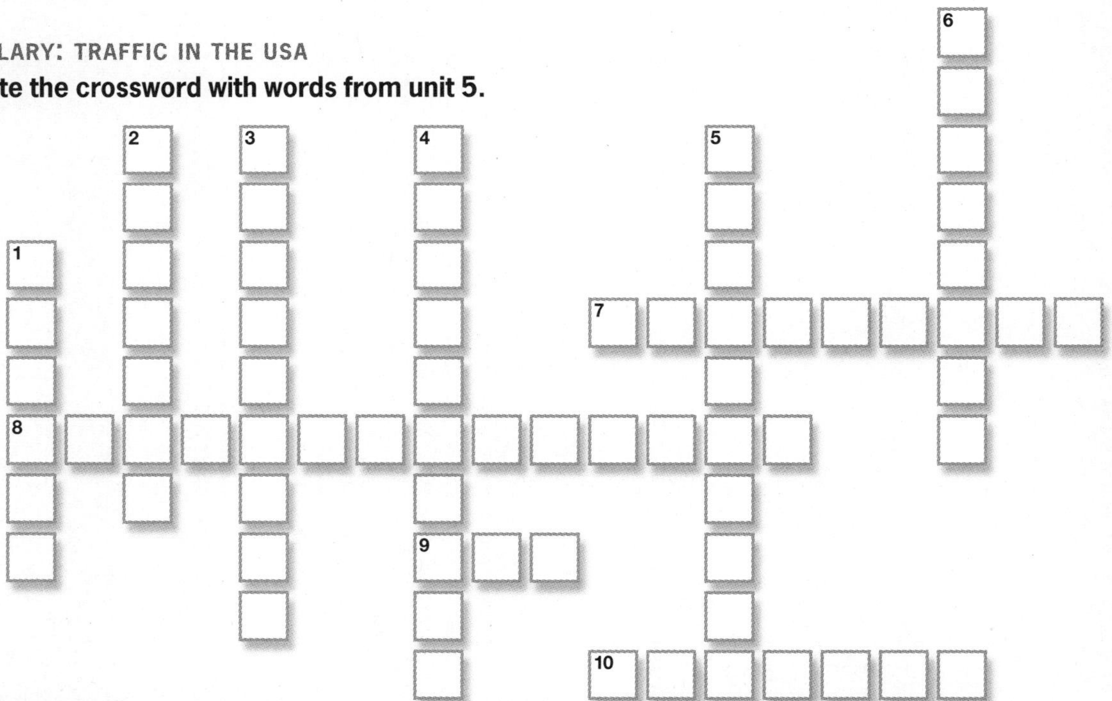

Across

7 If this happens, you can no longer drive your car.
8 In the USA you must be 16 to get one of these, and you need it to drive a car.
9 Read this to help you find the right road.
10 The police officer who might stop you if you're speeding on the highways.

Down

1 The George Washington in New York City and the Golden Gate in San Francisco, for example.
2 Cars and trucks on the roads.
3 There are more of these when there is a lot of snow and ice on the road.
4 In the USA it can be as low as 55 mph on some highways.
5 The kind of highway you take in the USA if you want to travel fast.
6 The time of day when there are a lot of cars and trucks on the roads because people are going to or leaving work.

6 PEOPLE AT WORK: PARTS OF A CAR

Find the ten parts of a car in the puzzle below. Then label the pictures with the words that you have found in the puzzle.

1 W □ □ □ S □ □ □ □ □

2 □ □ E □ L

3 B □ □ K □

4 □ □ E E R □ □ G W □ E E □

5 □ L □ □ C □

6 L □ G □ □ □

7 □ N □ □ N □

8 □ X H □ □ □ □

9 A □ □ □ L □ □ □ T □ □

10 □ Y □ □

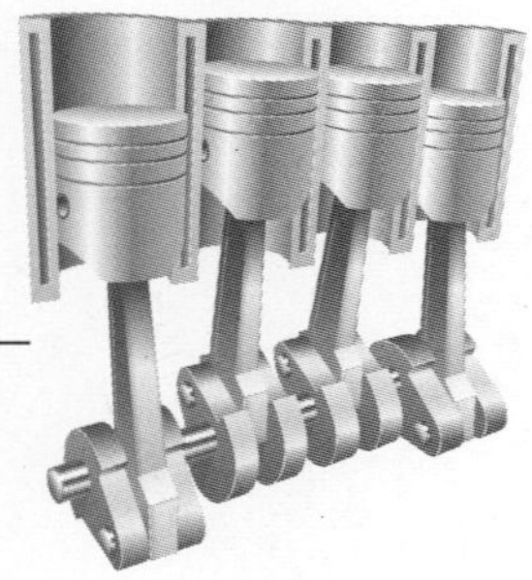

UNIT 6

The ups and downs of a teenager's life

1 ADVERBS

Write the adverb.

EXAMPLE nervous *nervously*

1 bad ____________________

2 sad ____________________

3 good ____________________

4 quick ____________________

5 easy ____________________

6 angry ____________________

7 dangerous ____________________

8 slow ____________________

9 happy ____________________

10 polite ____________________

11 helpful ____________________

12 regular ____________________

2 ADJECTIVE OR ADVERB?

Complete the sentences with an adjective or adverb from the list above.

EXAMPLE Chris was afraid the policewoman saw him shoplifting. He looked at her very *nervously*.

1 Sam was late for work so he ate his breakfast ________________.

2 The roads were very icy (*vereist*), and he was driving too fast. 'You're a ________________ driver!' said his girlfriend.

3 Sam knew the customer couldn't speak much English so he spoke very ________________ and clearly.

4 Chris always remembers to say thank you. He's a very ________________ boy.

5 Bina is very good at maths. I think she will do ________________ in the test.

6 Carol really loved her dog. She was very ________________ when it died.

7 Toni has a lot of arguments with her mum. Living at home is not ________________ for her.

8 Jo didn't learn much for the test. She did ________________ in the test.

9 Sam likes cars. He was very ________________ when he got a job as a mechanic.

10 There was a lot to do but Carol ________________ cleaned the bathroom for me.

11 My grandmother lives near me and I visit her ________________ once a week.

12 Bina gets so ________________ when her mum complains so they have a lot of arguments.

3

PRESENT PERFECT WITH *SINCE* OR *FOR*

Fill in the gaps using the words in brackets.

EXAMPLE How long *have you played volleyball*? (you play volleyball)

I *have played volleyball since last month*. (last month)

1 How long ________________________________? (have your job)

I ________________________________. (three months)

2 How long ________________________________? (Carol live in your street)

Carol ________________________________. (March)

3 How long ________________________________? (you be friends with Tony)

I ________________________________. (last year)

4 How long ________________________________? (argue with your mum)

I ________________________________. (six weeks)

5 How long ________________________________

__________? (be your brother ill)

My ________________________________

__________________. (Thursday)

6 How long ________________________________

__________? (they know your mum)

They ________________________________

__________________. (years)

They have been here since Christmas …

4

***SINCE* OR *FOR*?**

In six of these time expressions *since* is not correct. Which ones? Cross them out and correct them.

They have been here …

1 since last Sunday ____________________

2 since three months ____________________

3 since 21 January ____________________

4 since Christmas ____________________

5 since twenty minutes ____________________

6 since a long time ____________________

7 since a few minutes ____________________

8 since 10 o'clock ____________________

9 since five hours ____________________

10 since a week ____________________

5 PRESENT PERFECT WITH *SINCE* OR *FOR*

Complete the sentences with the correct form of the verb in brackets and *since* or *for*.

▶ EXAMPLE Sam met his girlfriend at Christmas. It's now 24 April.
He *has known* (know) her *for* four months.

Sam met his girlfriend at Christmas. It's now 24 April.
He *has known* (know) her *since* 24 April.

1 Chris and his friends came to the shopping centre at 10.30. It's now 12.30.

They ________________________ (be) there _________ two hours.

2 Chris met his friends John and Terry about three years ago. It's now 2006.

Chris _________________ (know) his friends _____________ 2003.

3 Valerie bought her bicycle three months ago. It's now August.

She ______________________ (have) her bike ____________ May.

4 When Chris moved to the house next to Jo's four years ago, Jo thought he was very attractive.

She still thinks so today.

Jo ___________________ (think) her neighbour is attractive ___________ four years.

5 Holly started her helpline in 1995.

She __________________ (have) her helpline ____________ 1995.

6 The police took the boys into their office at 11.40. It's now 12 noon.

The boys __________________ (be) with the police _________ twenty minutes.

7 Sam went on holiday three days ago. It is now Saturday.

Sam __________________ (be) away ____________ Wednesday.

6 VOCABULARY

Match the parts of the phrases in the boxes and then put them into two lists: the ups and the downs of a teenager's life. Then add two ups and two downs of your own.

~~unfair~~ • good • intolerant • angry • bad • an easy • my mobile • support from • a love

letter • my friends • job with good pay • ~~teachers~~ • marks • parents • people • friends • phone

UPS	DOWNS
______________	*unfair teachers*
______________	______________
______________	______________
______________	______________
______________	______________
______________	______________
______________	______________

7 EVERYDAY ENGLISH: PARTS OF A LETTER

Here is one of the readers' answers to Sam's letter. Match the sentence halves 1–8 with a–h.

Dear Sam

It's great that you have a job and that you enjoy working so hard.

1 But perhaps you're doing	c	**a**	see you regularly, too.
2 Your marks at school are	☐	**b**	very important.
3 They can help you get	☐	**c**	a bit too much.
4 And your girlfriend wants to	☐	**d**	carefully in other ways, too.
5 Why don't you just work	☐	**e**	two evenings a week or at weekends?
6 You can use your money more	☐	**f**	your mobile phone so much.
7 Don't buy expensive clothes, look in	☐	**g**	an interesting job later.
8 And don't use	☐	**h**	second-hand shops sometimes.

Good luck!

8 ADJECTIVES AND ADVERBS

Now put all the adjectives and adverbs from the letter above in the correct group. Add the missing adjectives and adverbs.

Adjectives	Adverbs
______________	______________
______________	______________
______________	______________
______________	______________
______________	______________
______________	______________
______________	______________
______________	______________
______________	______________

9 PEOPLE AT WORK

The youth worker can help with these problems which teenagers have. Fill in the missing words.

1 ______________ are good if you need them when you are ill but dangerous if they're just 'for fun'.

2 Children with parents who don't live together come from ______________ ______________.

3 Teenagers often have ______________ with their parents about their clothes or music.

4 Parents sometimes hit their children. It's a form of ______________.

5 People without work are ______________.

6 Some teenagers think shoplifting is a game, but it isn't. It's a ______________.

UNIT 7 English worldwide

1 VOCABULARY

Read this 'German' text and (circle) all the words that were originally English.

Funphone Halloween Disco

Chill-out mit der tollsten Party des Jahres. Verlost werden T-Shirts, Jeans, Anoraks, Gameboys, DVDs, Computerspiele und CDs. Ein bisschen Halloweenhorror muss auch sein, aber ‚just for fun'. Unsere Vampire und Goths bereiten keinen Stress. Und als Extrabonus wird das neue Funphone Videospiel-Handy F-Gage vorgeführt. Dieses Hightechhandy hat ein eingebautes Radio und einen MP3-Player. Auch für das Surfen im Internet sowie für das Senden und Empfangen von E-Mails und Multimediamessages ist F-Gage ausgerüstet.

Für Snacks wird gesorgt : Popcorn, Chips, Dips und Cola – so viel ihr wollt.

Euer Funphone Team lädt ein.

TIP *'Handy' ist zwar ein englisches Wort, bedeutet im Englischen jedoch etwas anderes. 'Handy' heißt* mobile (phone) *oder (in Amerika)* cell phone.

2 VOCABULARY

English as a world language? Match the words to the examples.

1	international travel	d	**a**	the internet
2	high-tech communication		**b**	German to English, French to Russian
3	old British colonies		**c**	schoolchildren in Europe, pilots
4	learners of English		**d**	by ship, by plane
5	a language designed by experts		**e**	film, theatre, TV, concerts
6	translation		**f**	Esperanto
7	entertainment		**g**	India, Pakistan, Nigeria

***Work with English* – Interactive**
Das Multimedia-Programm bietet vielfältige Übungen zu allen sprachlichen Bereichen an. Videosequenzen geben Einblick in das Leben in Großbritannien und trainieren das Hörverstehen. Man kann die eigene Sprache aufnehmen und beim Abspielen mit der Aussprache der *native speakers* vergleichen. Die CD-ROM enthält auch eine Nachschlagegrammatik und ein zweisprachiges Wörterbuch.
Weitere Vorzüge: Systematische Themenauswahl, automatische Fehlerkorrektur, individuelle Lerntipps, Leistungskontrolle.
So lernt man ganz selbstständig – zielgerichtet und nach eigenem Tempo.

Commercial Correspondence Elementary
Schrittweise und leicht verständlich vermittelt dieser Lehrgang, worauf es bei professioneller Geschäftskorrespondenz ankommt – ganz gleich, ob es um Anfragen, Angebote, Bestellungen, Bestätigungen oder Versandanzeigen geht. Die Lösungen zu den praktischen Übungen enthält der *Key.*

English for Emails
Der Band aus der Reihe *Short Courses* konzentriert sich auf die E-Mail-Korrespondenz. Den Kernwortschatz und die wichtigsten Wendungen kann man mithilfe vielfältiger Übungen erarbeiten, der *Answer Key* steht im Anhang.

Bestellungen der SSL-Lizenzen sind nur direkt beim Cornelsen Verlag mit **Schulstempel** oder **Immatrikulationsbescheinigung** möglich (keine Lieferung über den Buchhandel).

SSL Office 2003 Standard
Das Paket umfasst die Programme:
- Word 2003
- Excel 2003
- PowerPoint 2003
- Outlook 2003

Bestellkarte

Hiermit bestelle ich zur Lieferung wie umseitig ausgewiesen (per Nachnahme oder Bankeinzugsverfahren). Preis zuzüglich Versandkosten.

☐ **New Keep Going – Audio-CDs (2)**
Bestellnr. 28372 ◊ 24,95 €

☐ **Work with English – Interactive**
CD-ROM für Multimedia-PC ab Windows 95.
Bestellnr. 61477 ◊ 49,95 €

Commercial Correspondence Elementary

☐ **Practice Book**
72 Seiten. Bestellnr. 19926 7,95 €

☐ **Key**
Bestellnr. 19934 4,– €

☐ **English for Emails**
64 Seiten. Bestellnr. 18784 12,50 €

Gewünschtes bitte in dem entsprechenden Kästchen deutlich ankreuzen. Alle Titel können auch durch den Buchhandel zum Ladenpreis ohne Versandkosten bezogen werden.
Preisstand 1.1.2005. Änderungen vorbehalten. ◊ = Unverbindliche Preisempfehlung.

Bestellkarte

Hiermit bestelle ich zur Lieferung wie umseitig ausgewiesen (per Nachnahme oder Bankeinzugsverfahren). Preis zuzüglich Versandkosten.

Wichtiger Hinweis zur Bestellung:
Im Falle einer Bestellung erhalten Sie von uns ein Paket mit einer vorläufigen Lizenz, den Lizenzvereinbarungen und einem Bestellformular für die Software-CD-ROM, die direkt von *Microsoft* an den Kunden ausgeliefert wird. Dieses Bestellformular können Sie vollständig ausgefüllt an die im Paket hinterlegte Fax-Nr. senden oder online unter Angabe Ihrer im Paket beigefügten PID-Nr. (Produktidentifikations-Nr.) beim *Student Licence Center* von *Microsoft* ordern. Eine detaillierte Beschreibung über die Verfahrensweise finden Sie im Paket. Der Lieferumfang umfasst die persönliche Lizenz, die mit der Unterschrift des Bestellers gültig wird, und eine CD-ROM mit der Software.

☐ **SSL Office 2003 Standard** (wird bereits mit Datenträger geliefert)
Bestellnr. 927180 ◊ 169,— €

Gewünschtes bitte in dem entsprechenden Kästchen deutlich ankreuzen.
Preisstand 1.1.2005. Änderungen vorbehalten. ◊ = Unverbindliche Preisempfehlung.

Bitte in Druckschrift komplett ausfüllen

Name / Vorname — Alter des Schülers

Straße / Hausnummer

Postleitzahl / Ort

Datum / Unterschrift (der/des Erziehungsberechtigten)

Ich bestelle zur Lieferung:

☐ per Nachnahme (Preis zzgl. Versandkosten und 3,32 € Nachnahmegebühr)

☐ per Bankeinzug (Preis zzgl. Versandkosten)

Kontonummer

Bankleitzahl

Name des Kontoinhabers

Datum / Unterschrift des Kontoinhabers

BK 310

Bitte freimachen

Antwortkarte

Cornelsen

Cornelsen Verlag

14328 Berlin

Bitte in Druckschrift komplett ausfüllen

Name / Vorname — Alter des Schülers

Straße / Hausnummer

Postleitzahl / Ort

Datum / Unterschrift (der/des Erziehungsberechtigten)

Ich bestelle zur Lieferung:

☐ per Nachnahme (Preis zzgl. Versandkosten und 3,32 € Nachnahmegebühr)

☐ per Bankeinzug (Preis zzgl. Versandkosten)

Kontonummer

Bankleitzahl

Name des Kontoinhabers

Datum / Unterschrift des Kontoinhabers

BK 313

Bitte freimachen

Antwortkarte

Cornelsen

Cornelsen Verlag

14328 Berlin

THE *WILL* FUTURE

3 Complete the sentences with *will / 'll* or *won't* and the correct verb from the box.

Heike has decided to spend a year in Australia, and is now thinking about what the future will be like.

meet • laugh • miss • learn • understand

1 I hope I ______________________________ a lot of new English words.

2 I hope the Australians ______________________________ my English.

3 I hope the kids at school ______________________________ at me.

4 I hope I ______________________________ some interesting people.

5 I hope I ______________________________ my family and friends too much.

This is what her family and friends say about her.

make • celebrate • go • forget • have

7 I think Heike ______________________________ a wonderful time.

8 I think she ______________________________ new friends easily. She's so friendly.

9 I'm sure that she ______________________________ skiing a lot this January.

10 Perhaps she ______________________________ Christmas at the beach.

11 I hope she ______________________________ her German.

THE *WILL* FUTURE

4 It isn't so easy to get ready to leave home for a year! Heike's friends Martina and Sharon have offered to help. Write sentences using the box.

I'll We'll	write phone buy celebrate visit send come	an address list. you the school magazine. your friend Sam every week. you a lot of emails. you some books about Australia. your birthday with friends. to the airport to meet you in July. your family.

______________________________ ______________________________

______________________________ ______________________________

______________________________ ______________________________

______________________________ ______________________________

______________________________ ______________________________

______________________________ ______________________________

THE *WILL* FUTURE

5 Some friends are talking about what they think will happen in the future. Write sentences about the topics below using the words in the boxes.

~~clean houses, cook~~	be warmer, rain a lot	
live longer but not have enough money for houses and food	fruits and vegetables stay fresh longer, taste better	
use solar energy *(Solarenergie)* and not petrol *(Benzin)*	often have to retrain, learn new jobs	many terrorists, not safe to fly

ROBOTS In the future, *they will clean our houses and cook for us.*

JOBS In the future, people ______________________________
____

CARS In the future, cars ______________________________
____

CLIMATE In the future, it ______________________________
____

PEOPLE OVER 65 In the future, they ______________________________
____

OUR FOOD In the future, ______________________________
____

TERRORISTS In the future, there ______________________________
____

PARAPHRASING

6 Read the explanations below and then complete the puzzle.

1. This is a person who isn't a child or teenager.
2. This is where you go if you are ill.
3. This is a place where you can buy food and clothes outside.
4. This is someone who knows a lot about something.
5. This is the room where you wash.
6. This is not the past or the present but the … .
7. This person is like a driver of planes and helicopters.

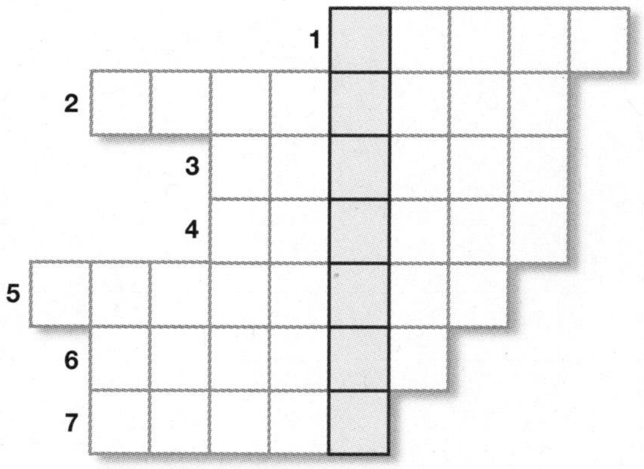

The mystery word is where you go to travel on a plane.

7

THE *WILL* FUTURE

Karin's boss has left some notes for an email to a Japanese tour guide *(Reiseführer)*. Complete the sentences using the verbs from the box.

> print out (x 2) • plan • ~~welcome~~ • make • help • give • phone

- um 15 Uhr die Gruppe im Hotel begrüßen
- jedem Gast einen Stadtplan geben
- das Abendessen für 19 Uhr planen
- Reservierungen für eine Stadtrundfahrt machen
- das Programm für die drei Tage ausdrucken
- den Gästen mit Theater- und Konzertkarten helfen
- Herrn Kamoto eine Gruppenrechnung beim Checkout ausdrucken
- Taxis rufen, um sie zum Flughafen zu bringen

1 *We'll welcome you at the hotel at 3 p.m.*

2 We ________________________ each guest a city map.

3 ________________________ dinner for 7 p.m.

4 ______________________________________ for a city tour.

5 ______________________________________ a programme for the three days.

6 ____ with theatre and concert tickets.

7 ________________________________ a group bill for you when you check out.

8 ________________________________ for taxis to take you to the airport.

8

PEOPLE AT WORK: A HOTEL RESERVATION

Complete this email about a hotel reservation with the words from the box.

> smoking • shower • pool • breakfast • nights • double • fitness • price

Dear Sir or Madam

I would like to book a ____________[1] room with ______________[2] or bath for three ___________[3] from 21 to 24 March. We would like a non_______________[4] room. Is there a ______________[5] centre and swimming _____________[6] in the hotel? Does the price of €75 include a full _________________[7]? Please confirm *(bestätigen)* the ____________[8] and hotel reservation.

Thank you.

Yours faithfully

UNIT 8 Do you want to be super(wo)man?

1 VOCABULARY: BODY PARTS

Write the English words for these body parts in the crossword.

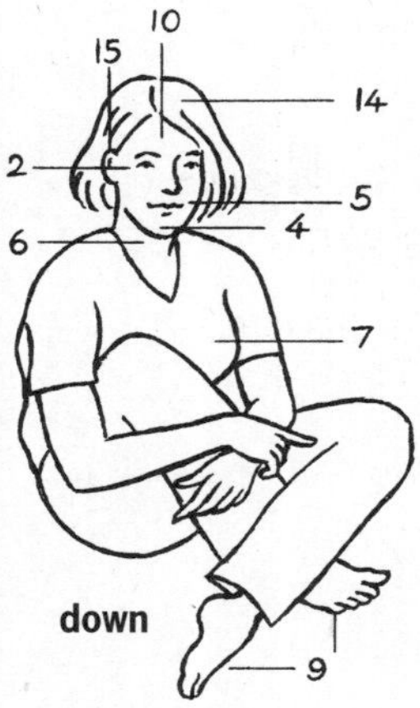

down

across

2 *IF* SENTENCES TYPE 1

Put the words in the correct order to make sentences.

1 If / plastic surgery / want / you ______

it / expensive / be / very / will ______

2 When / finishes / the doctor / with this patient ______

______ you / see / he'll ______

3 Dan / cosmetic surgery / if / on his nose / has ______

won't / know / his mother / him ______

4 a nice girl / meets / Dan / if ______

at his nose / she / look / won't ______

5 finishes / Jane / school / when ______

will / she / as a nurse / train ______

6 he / finishes / when / his job interview ______

have to / he'll / a test / do ______

IF SENTENCES TYPE 1

3 **Susan is arguing with her boyfriend. What does she say? Use the box to write her answers.**

If you	do, don't,	I my mum	'll will won't	be angry with us both. go with Max. phone or email you. stop seeing you.

1 **ALAN** I'm not going to go to the dance next Wednesday.

SUSAN ______________________________

2 **ALAN** I'd like to have purple hair.

SUSAN ______________________________

3 **ALAN** I hope to spend the next holidays in the USA.

SUSAN ______________________________

4 **ALAN** I don't really want to help you tidy up your room.

SUSAN ______________________________

EVERYDAY ENGLISH: ACCIDENTS

4 **What would you say in an English-speaking country? Use the present perfect of the verbs in the box to translate these sentences.**

cut • lose • hurt • break • have an accident

▶ **EXAMPLE** Sie haben sich am Fuß geschnitten. *I've cut my foot.*

1 Sie haben sich an der Hand verletzt. *I've* ______________________

2 Sie haben einen Zahn verloren. *I've* ______________________

3 Sie glauben, Sie haben ein Bein gebrochen. *I think I've* ______________________

4 Ihr Freund hat sich den Kopf verletzt. *My friend has* ______________________

5 Zwei Freunde haben ein Autounfall gehabt. *Two friends* ______________________

6 Das Kind hat sich am Kinn und Ohr geschnitten. *The child has* ______________________

Match these answers to the questions above.

a ☐ I'll give you the name of a good dentist (*Zahnarzt*).

b ☐ That's awful! Were they hurt?

c ☐ Can you move (*bewegen*) your fingers?

d ☐ If you can't walk, go to the doctor for an X-ray.

e ☐ I'll wash them and put some medicine on them.

f ☐ Oh no! Is he unconscious?

5 GOING TO FUTURE

Look at the pictures and say what they are going to do.

▶ **EXAMPLE** They *are going to play* tennis.

1 He ______________________________

______________ his shirt.

2 She ______________________________

______________ an X-ray.

3 They ______________________________

______________ a cake.

4 They ______________________________

______________ with the band.

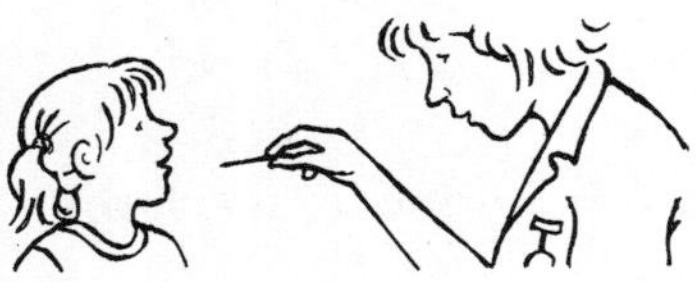

5 The nurse ______________________________

______________ her temperature.

6 PEOPLE AT WORK / *IF* OR *WHEN*?

Carmen writes an email to a friend of hers after a hard day at work in Newgrove Hospital. Complete the text with the words from the box.

laboratory • medicine • take • knee • shift • ward • temperature • tests

Hi Jane

It was a busy day today, but that's typical for the children's __________ 1 at Newgrove Hospital. There are a lot of children who need care. There's a little boy who has leukemia and has to have so many blood __________ 2. Every day when we __________ 3 his blood for the test he cries (*weinen*) but if they don't check his blood in the ______________ 4, they won't know what ______________ 5 to give him. Most of the kids think it's fun when we take their ______________ 6 every morning. But they almost always cry when it's time for them to have their injections.

Next week I'm going to work the night ____________ 7. I get tired but I can sleep for a few hours if there aren't any problems. How was the operation on your ______________ 8 ? Don't forget I want to go walking in Wales with you next month, but only if you can walk well then, of course.

Love,
Carmen

Without looking back at the text, put in *when* or *if*.

1 The little boy cries every day __________ we take his blood for a test.

2 __________ they don't check his blood, they won't know what medicine to give him.

3 The kids think it's fun __________ we take their temperature every morning.

4 They always cry __________ it's time for their injections.

5 I can sleep for a few hours __________ there aren't any problems.

6 We'll go hiking in Wales __________ you can walk well then.

7

PEOPLE AT WORK / *GOING TO* FUTURE

A little girl has just come into Newgrove Hospital after a car accident with a broken arm and leg. She also has cuts on her head. How are the people at the hospital going to help her? Complete the sentences with the verb in the *going to* future.

EXAMPLE They*'re going to wash* (wash) her bloody clothes.

1 They __________________________ (take) photos of her arm and leg.

2 A nurse __________________________ (take) blood , then send it for a test.

3 The doctors __________________________ (give) her an injection to make her sleep.

4 The doctors __________________________ (do) an operation on her arm and leg. Then they__________________________ (put) a plaster on her arm and leg.

5 After the operation, Carmen __________________________ (wash) the cuts on her head again and __________________________ (put) some medicine on them.

6 They __________________________(cook) good food for her after the operation.

8

PEOPLE AT WORK / *WILL* FUTURE

Where will they do the things described in the sentences above?

laundry • laboratory • X-ray department • ward • operating theatre • kitchens

EXAMPLE They will wash her bloody clothes in the *laundry*.

1 ____

2 ____

3 ____

4 ____

____

5 ____

____

6 ____

UNIT 9 If I had the chance ...

1 VOCABULARY: JOBS

Which words go together?

An employee does this before or after he/she has found a job.

look	money
write	a letter of application
go	for a job
have	hard
fill in	a holiday
apply for	a job
work	a form
earn	for a job interview

look for a job ______

______

______

______

______

______

______

______

An employer or a person with his/her own business does this.

rent (*mieten*)	a company
set up	people
interview	customers
hire	the work of his/her staff
work	staff
start up	a website
find and contact	an office
check	overtime often

______

______

______

______

______

______

______

______

TIP Bei Konditionalsätzen kann man entweder mit dem *if*-Satz oder mit dem Hauptsatz beginnen.
Im einen Fall setzt man ein Komma, im anderen nicht:
If I had a million euros, I would travel around the world. (Komma)
I would travel around the world if I had a million euros. (kein Komma)
Und denken Sie daran: Im *if*-Satz steht kein *would*!

2 *IF* SENTENCES TYPE 2

What did Jenny's customers think about their secret wishes before they hired Jenny to help them? Put the words in the sentences in the right order.

1 if / the chance / had / I *If* ______

a Formula 1 car / drive / would / I *I* ______

2 I / if / the money / had *If* ______

my own CD / would / I / record *I* ______

3 a good band / if / I / knew *If* ______________________________

I / them / ask / would / to play / for my boyfriend / 'Happy Birthday' ______________

____

4 my girlfriend / told me / if / her secret dream *If* ______________________

____

Jenny Parsons / ask / to help me / fulfil it / would / I *I* ______________________

____

5 I / to fulfil my wish / ask / would / Jenny Parsons *I* ______________________

______________ I / a lot of money / if / had *if* ______________________

6 a bungee-jump / do / from a helicopter / I / would *I* ______________________

____

if / knew / I / to do it / where *if* ______________________________

IF **SENTENCES TYPE 2**

3 **Jenny's younger brother, Ted, who works in an office, is thinking about getting an extra part-time job as a gardener. She is giving him advice. Fill in the correct form of the verb in her sentences.**

EXAMPLE If you *took* (take) a sandwich to work, you *wouldn't spend* (not / spend) so much money.

1 If you __________ (do) outdoor work, you __________ (get) a lot of fresh air.

2 And if you __________ (do) some physical work, you ______________ (feel) better.

3 If you ______________ (work) longer hours, you ______________ (be) very tired in the evening.

4 If you ______________ (eat) lunch in the canteen and not your favourite restaurant, you ________________ (not / need) so much money for lunches.

5 If you ________________ (go) to work by bicycle, you ____________________ (not / need) so much money for the bus.

6 If you __________ (get) a part-time job during your holidays, you ____________________ (not / have) time to go to Spain with your girlfriend.

7 If you __________ (do) an extra job after your office job, you ____________________ (not / have) enough time for your hobbies.

8 If you __________ (do) garden work, you ____________________ (learn) something very useful for your own garden one day.

9 If you ______________ (not / buy) so many clothes and CDs, you ______________ (have) more money at the end of the month.

10 If you ______________ (ask)your girlfriend, perhaps she __________________ (pay) for half of your concert tickets.

4 *IF* SENTENCES TYPE 2

Ted is thinking about the advice his sister gave him. He decides to make lists for himself. Use the ideas above to complete his lists.

▶ **EXAMPLE** I'd save money if *I took* a sandwich to work.

A I'd save money if …

1 ______________________________ by bicycle.

2 ______________________________ in the canteen.

3 ______________________________ so many clothes and CDs.

4 ______________________________ my girlfriend to pay for half of our concert tickets.

B If I took the gardening job, it would be good because …

1 ______________________________ fresh air.

2 ______________________________ better.

3 ______________________________ something useful for my own garden.

C If I took the gardening job, it would be bad because …

1 ______________________________ tired in the evening.

2 ______________________________ enough free time for my hobbies.

3 ______________________________ time to go to Spain with my girlfriend.

5 VOCABULARY: FINDING A JOB

Ted got his gardening job. Now he's trying to help a friend who can't find a job. Complete his email with the following words.

needed • newspaper • looked • try to help • staff • unemployed • hire • started

Hi Marty
Sorry you're having such a hard time finding a good job. If there weren't so many ______________ 1 people, it would be easier to find one, I'm sure. Maybe if you ______________ 2 in different newspapers or on the internet, you would find more jobs. I can ask at my company for you, but I think if they wanted to ______________ 3 more staff, they would put an advert in the ______________ 4, or at least on the company message board. I've just ______________ 5 an extra part-time job as a gardener because I never have enough money to do the things I want. If my gardening employer ______________ 6 more people, I'd tell him about you. But I know he isn't going to hire any new ______________ 7 soon. If I had a little more time, I'd ______________ 8 you look for the right kind of job.

Maybe I'll have a good idea.
All the best
Ted

EVERYDAY ENGLISH: JOB INTERVIEWS

6 **Jenny wants to hire a third employee. Look at the sentences and decide which ones she says and which ones the people who apply for the job say. Mark them J for Jenny, P for people.**

▶ **EXAMPLE** Thank you for coming for a job interview. *J*

1 I'm very glad you liked my letter of application. ☐
2 Have you got any other qualifications? ☐
3 What exactly would my duties be if I took this job? ☐
4 You would answer the telephone and look after the post. ☐
5 How long have you worked for your present employer? ☐
6 I've just finished a course in business at Gwynt Vocational College. ☐
7 Why do you think you'd be good for this job? ☐
8 How many days holiday would I get every year? ☐
9 When could you start? ☐
10 I'm very flexible and I like doing different kinds of work. ☐
11 I don't like working for big companies. I'd really like to work for a small firm. ☐
12 Why do you want to leave your present job? ☐

EVERYDAY ENGLISH: TALKING ABOUT JOBS

7 **Think of the jobs you have learned about up to now, and complete the sentences.**

nurse • ~~painter~~ • roofer • waitress • kindergarten teacher • telephonist • shop assistant • bricklayer • cook • bank clerk • airport worker • electrician • plumber

▶ **EXAMPLE** *If I was a painter*, people would ask me to change the colour of their house.

1 ________________________, people would ask me for help with their money problems.
2 ________________________, I'd prepare lovely meals.
3 ________________________, I'd work with very small children.
4 ________________________, I'd sell people things.
5 ________________________, I'd take temperatures and give injections.
6 ________________________, I'd look through travellers' bags.
7 ________________________, people would ask me to repair their sink units and toilets.
8 ________________________, I'd check the wiring and install lights.
9 ________________________, I'd work on the top of buildings.
10 ________________________, I'd give people their food.
11 ________________________, I'd build walls.
12 ________________________, people would call me and I would take messages for them.

UNIT 10

Emergency!

1

SIMPLE PAST – SAYING WHAT HAPPENED IN THE PAST

Jenny was in a car accident yesterday. Luckily, nobody was badly hurt. Complete the sentences about what happened, by using the simple past of the verb.

EXAMPLE Jenny, her brother Ted and his girlfriend *wanted* (want) to go to a birthday party in Reading yesterday.

1 They ______________ (leave) their house in London at about 5 pm.

2 The accident ______________ (happen) at about 6 pm.

3 A truck ____________________ (not / see) them and ______________ (hit) Jenny's car.

4 Ted's arm and leg ______________ (be) hurt, Jenny's face and hands ______________ (be) cut.

5 The truck driver ______________ (call) an ambulance on his mobile phone.

6 The paramedics ____________ (give) them first aid, then _____________ (take) them to hospital.

2

PAST CONTINUOUS – SAYING WHAT SOMEONE WAS DOING WHEN SOMETHING HAPPENED

A policeman is asking Jenny questions about the accident. Use the words in brackets to answer his questions.

EXAMPLE
POLICEMAN Where exactly were you when the accident happened?
JENNY (drive on the M25 / near Heathrow Airport)
We were driving on the M25, near Heathrow Airport.

1 POLICEMAN Was there anyone else with you?
JENNY (Yes, my brother's girlfriend. She / sleep / in the back)
Yes, my brother's girlfriend. She ____ .

2 POLICEMAN How fast were you going?
JENNY (go / about 70 km per hour)
We ____ .

3 POLICEMAN That's quite slow.
JENNY (Yes / but rain very hard)
Yes, but it ____ .

4 POLICEMAN Was your brother using his mobile phone?
JENNY (No, he wasn't. We / listen to music / car radio)
No, he wasn't. We ____ .

5 POLICEMAN What was the truck doing when it hit you?
JENNY (It / try to drive around us)
It ____ .

6 POLICEMAN Was he driving fast?
JENNY (No, he / drive not fast, but / rain)
No, he ____________________________ , but it ____________________________
and it was difficult to see or stop quickly.

3 QUESTIONS IN THE SIMPLE PAST AND PAST CONTINUOUS

What are typical questions for a policeman to ask after a car accident? Complete these with the verbs in the simple past or past continuous. You can check back in Exercises 1 and 2.

1 When ________________ the accident ________________? (happen)

2 How fast ________________ you ________________? (drive)

3 ________________ anyone hurt? (be)

4 ________________ you ________________ on your mobile phone? (talk)

5 What ________________ the other car ________________? (do)

6 Why ________________ you ________________ the other car? (not / see)

7 ________________ it ________________? (rain)

8 What ________________ the other people in the car ________________? (do)

4 SIMPLE PAST AND PAST CONTINUOUS

When the shark attacked Dennis there were a lot of people on the beach. The police asked five people what they were doing when they saw the attack. Complete the questions and answers with the correct forms of the verbs.

PEDRO I ________________ a cold beer when the shark ________________. (have, attack)

MARGIE I ________________ sandwiches. When I ________________ the attack, I ________________ the rescue helicopter. (make, see, call)

DENNIS'S SISTER I ________________ a scream while I ________________ beach volleyball. (hear, play)

DENNIS'S MOTHER When the accident ________________, I ________________ a magazine. (happen, read)

The lifeguard ________________ to some people. When he ________________ someone screaming, he ________________ his equipment. (talk, hear, grab)

AN OLD MAN I ________________ in the sun. When I heard the screams, I ________________ and ________________ at the water. (lie, sit up, look)

SIMPLE PAST AND PAST CONTINUOUS – READING STORIES

5 **John and Bob told their stories of dangerous situations on 'Emergency Call' and talked about their big and little emergencies. Find their two stories in the eight sentences. Write the numbers of the sentences in the correct order next to the person in each story.**

JOHN [4] [ ] [ ] [ ] BOB, AN ELECTRICIAN [5] [ ] [ ] [ ]

1 He got a shock and fell to the ground unconscious.
2 Luckily the tiger ran away.
3 Timmy, aged 6, was playing in his room when he heard the crash.
4 John was walking in the Himalayas when he saw a tiger.
5 Bob was repairing the wiring in an old building when lightning struck.
6 He was very surprised but he didn't scream and run away.
7 He was already holding his camera so he quietly took a picture of it.
8 Timmy found the electrician on the floor and called the doctor next door.

Now answer the questions.

1 What was John doing when he saw the tiger?

____

2 Why was it easy to take a picture of it?

____

3 What was Bob doing when lightning struck?

____

4 What was Timmy Jones doing when he heard the crash?

____

EVERYDAY ENGLISH: TELEPHONE LANGUAGE

6 **Donald calls Smith Company and wants to speak to John Smith. Complete the conversation.**

Good morning, Smith Company. ______________ help you?

Can ______________ John Smith please?

Could you ______________ your name please?

__________ is Donald O'Connell. Is John Smith __________ ?

Sorry, but he's ______________ at the moment. Can I ______________ message?

Yes, please ask him to ______________ after 8 pm on 219 485 0567?

Of course, Mr O'Connell. 219 485 0567. I______________ him the message.

Thank ______________. Goodbye.

7 EVERYDAY ENGLISH – TRANSLATING A PHONE CALL

Translate this telephone conversation into English.

RECEPTIONIST Guten Tag, Thomas and Sons. Wie kann ich Ihnen helfen?

____

JULIA Hier spricht Julia Brown. Ich rufe wegen eines Termins mit Mark Thomas an. Kann ich bitte mit Herrn Thomas sprechen?

____

____

RECEPTIONIST Bleiben Sie dran. … Auf seiner Leitung wird gerade gesprochen und er hat gleich einen Termin. Können Sie später noch mal anrufen?

____

____

JULIA Wann ist er zurück? ______________________________

RECEPTIONIST Er kommt in zwei Stunden zurück. ______________________________

JULIA Gut. Ich rufe später zurück. Vielen Dank.

____

RECEPTIONIST Danke. Wiederhören. ______________________________

8 PEOPLE AT WORK: OFFICE WORK

Yesterday morning Helen Thompson, Girl Friday at the zoo, was very busy. Fill in the words in the boxes 1–5. Then use the letters in the grey boxes to find out what she didn't have time to write.

1 She ☐☐☐☐ her boss's diary.

2 She ☐☐☐☐ coffee.

3 She ☐☐☐☐ and took a lot of phone calls.

4 She ☐☐☐ the filing.

5 She ☐☐☐☐☐☐☐☐ some Japanese guests to the zoo.

6 She didn't have any time to write an ☐☐☐☐☐.

9 PEOPLE AT WORK: WELCOMING A VISITOR

Use the words in the box to complete the questions to a visitor in an office.

coat • journey • seat • tell

Did you have a good ______________________?

Can I take your ______________________?

I'll ______________________ Mr Schmidt that you're here.

Please have a ______________________.

UNIT 11 # A job downunder

1 VOCABULARY: WORK AS AN AU PAIR

Jill is telling another au pair, Terry, about her job. Group the activities under morning, afternoon and evening. She only does housework and babysitting sometimes.

clean the house • collect children from school • do the ironing • do the washing • get breakfast for the kids • help children with homework • help the kids wash and dress • look after the kids if their parents go out • make dinner for the family • prepare a lunch packet for the kids • take the kids to school

In the morning I always have to .... .

____

____

____

____

And sometimes I have to .... .

____

____

____

In the afternoon I usually have to .... .

____

____

In the evening I sometimes

____

____

2 *HAVE TO*

Jill wants to find out what Terry has to do for her family. Complete the dialogue with (*don't* +) *have to* + the verbs from exercise 1.

▶ EXAMPLE

JILL *Do* you *have to work* hard?

TERRY No, I *don't*. But I *have to do* a lot of different things.

JILL ________ you ______________________ [1] the kids to school?

TERRY No, I ________ [2]. Their father takes them when he goes to work.

But I ______________________ [3] them breakfast.

JILL ________ you ______________________ [4] the kids wash and dress?

TERRY No, I ________ [5]. They're older than your kids.

But sometimes I ______________________ [6] a blouse for one of the girls to wear.

JILL ________ you ______________________ [7] a lunch packet?

TERRY No, I ________ [8]. They eat in the school canteen. But I often ______________________

______________________ [9] a snack for them when they come home.

JILL ________ you ______________________ [10] housework?

TERRY Well, I ______________________[11] the washing and ironing. But I ______________________[12] the cleaning. A woman comes on Monday and Wednesday to do that. She does everything. The kids ______________________[13] their own room. Aren't they lucky?

HAVE TO

3 **On Monday morning, Jill found this note from the woman she works for as an au pair.**

> *Good morning Jill*
> *I don't have to work tomorrow, so you can have the day off. But could you possibly help me in the evening. I'm having friends over for dinner. I'll do the shopping and cooking, but it would be great if you could help clean up later, and play with the kids so we can talk. I'll talk to you this evening!*
> *Karen*

So on Tuesday Jill went with her friend Terry to the beach.
On Wednesday she wrote this email to her boyfriend Davey in the Outback.
Fill in *had to / didn't have to / Did you have to* + the verb given.

I had a great day on Tuesday. Karen ______________________[1] (work) so she was at home and I ______________________[2] (look after) the kids. Terry and I went to the beach for the day. It was great fun, but the sun was really hot and we ______________________[3] (use) lots of sunscreen. Terry ______________________[4] (go) home at 4 because she ______________________[5] (help) the kids at her house with their homework. She ______________________[6] (make) dinner for the family too. But I ______________________[7] (be) home until 7 pm, so after the beach I went to the cinema. Karen had friends over for dinner, so after dinner I ______________________[8] (help) clean up. I also ______________________[9] (play) with the kids so their parents could talk with their friends.

How was your week? I hope you ______________________[10] (look for) so many lost sheep again like last week.

Write soon!

Love Jill

1 selected

MUST AND *CAN* – PAST AND FUTURE FORMS

4 **Jill and her employer are talking about work. Complete the sentences with the past or future forms of the verbs in brackets.**

KAREN Jill, you must help the kids with their homework this afternoon.

JILL OK, Karen. But I <u>had to help</u> [1] (must help) them for three hours yesterday, too.

KAREN I know. And you ______________________ [2] (must help) them tomorrow. They've got big tests on Friday! But you can go to the beach a couple of days next week.

JILL Thanks Karen! It was great that I ______________________ [3] (can go) to the beach last Tuesday. I'll tell Terry that I ______________________ [4] (can go) to the beach next Tuesday too.

Now Davey and his employer are talking about work.

JOHN Davey, can you fill up the quad with petrol? It's almost empty.

DAVEY I know. I ______________________ [5] (can not fill it up) yesterday because I didn't have time. I can't do it today, because I have to help Tom with some welding. But I know that I ______________________ [6] (can fill up) early tomorrow morning.

JOHN No, there's no welding today because we must look for those 200 missing sheep over near Blue River.

DAVEY We ______________________ [7] (must look for) them yesterday too, but it was raining a lot and we had to stop.

JOHN If we don't find them today, we ______________________ [8] (must look for) them early tomorrow morning. There's more rain coming.

Grammar

■ *Should* and *may*

You **should** look for a better job.
Du solltest dich nach einer besseren Stelle umsehen.

You **shouldn't** drive so fast on these roads.
Auf diesen Straßen solltest du nicht so schnell fahren.

That **shouldn't** be a problem for you.
Das sollte kein Problem für dich sein.

You **may** smoke in that room.
In dem Raum darf man rauchen.

He **may** go to Stockholm next month.
Möglicherweise fährt er nächste Woche nach Stockholm.

- *Should / shouldn't* drücken wie das deutsche ‚sollte' meistens einen Ratschlag oder eine Empfehlung aus. Sie können auch zum Ausdruck einer festen Überzeugung gebraucht werden, wie oben im dritten Satz.
- *May / may not* wird entweder mit ‚können' im Sinne von ‚dürfen' oder mit Umschreibungen wie ‚vielleicht' oder ‚möglicherweise' übersetzt.
- *May / may not* kann auch ‚dürfen' bedeuten, also eine Erlaubnis oder ein Verbot.

5 *HAVE TO, MUST, CAN, COULD, BE ABLE TO, MAY, SHOULD* – NEGATIVE FORMS

Davey's boss is talking to him about work. Read the sentences and choose the correct way to complete the sentence. The grammar box on p. 54 may help you.

1 We *should / shouldn't* go to bed early because we have to start work very early in the morning.
2 We *were / weren't* able to fix the fence because the hole was too big.
3 You *have to / don't have to* check the fence today because I can't do it.
4 You *must / mustn't* forget to take some medicine because some of the sheep may be ill.
5 You *may / may not* have enough petrol because I had to drive 300 kilometers yesterday.
6 We *were / weren't* able to find all of the lost sheep because they weren't very far away.
7 You *may / may not* have problems with the car, because we couldn't get a new battery.
8 You *should / shouldn't* forget your mobile phone, because there may be a problem with the dingos.

6 PEOPLE AT WORK: WORKING AS A SOCIAL VOLUNTEER

Jill has a job as a social volunteer and works with children who have the learning difficulty, Attention Deficit Disorder. Match the sentence parts to find out what she does and what she doesn't do. Look at the text in your book on p. 108 if you need help.

1 The children should ☐
2 Jill is just a volunteer and not really qualified, ☐
3 Jill mustn't be too strict ☐
4 Jill has to keep an eye ☐
5 Jill is able to ☐
6 Jill can see herself ☐

a build up a strong relationship with some of the kids.
b in this job one day.
c on the ADD children.
d run and jump and let off steam.
e so she can't teach the children.
f with the children.

UNIT 12 Personalities & the media

1 VOCABULARY: MEDIA

Fill in the words for these popular media.

1 They have pictures and articles about many different things.
2 Here's where you can see the Simpsons.
3 People often listen to this when they are working in the kitchen or driving a car. It's good for music, news, the weather report, traffic information and many other things.
4 If you need information about a special theme, just turn on your computer and look it up here.
5 Every day you can read about the latest news here. You can also find information about things like cinemas and concerts.

1 _ _ _ _ _ _ _ _ _
2 _ _ _ _ _ _ _ _ _ _
3 _ _ _ _ _
4 _ _ _ _ _ _ _ _
5 _ _ _ _ _ _ _ _ _

2 VOCABULARY: TELEVISION

Look at what's on BBC, then use one of the phrases in the box to complete the sentence correctly.

- documentary programmes
- news broadcasts
- primetime programmes
- talk shows
- entertainment programmes
- sports programmes

1 *Top of the Pops* and *Entertainment Now* are ______________________ ______________________.

2 *EastEnders, All About Me* and *Absolutely Fabulous* are ______________________ ______________________.

BBC1

6.00 am Breakfast. (S) (T) Followed by **The National Lottery Daily Play.** (401216)
9.00 Fast and Dangerous. Documentary reporting on the dangerous high-speed pursuits of criminals by police drivers which have resulted in the deaths of 148 people in the past six years. (S) (T) (52987)
11.00 Top of the Pops. (R) (S) (T) (62884)
11.30 To Buy or Not to Buy. (R) (S) (T) Followed by **News and Weather.** (2736)
12.00 Trading Treasures. (R) (S) (T) (32910)
12.30 Bargain Hunt. (R) (S) (T) (67194)
1.00 News and Weather. (T) (48620)
1.30 Regional News. (56614991)
1.40 Neighbours. (S) (T) (83839620)
2.05 What the Romans Did for Us. Adam Hart-Davis chronicles the Romans' withdrawal from Britain. (R) (S) (T) (16047338)
3.25 CBBC. Tweenies. (R) (S) (T) (6608804) **3.45** Arthur. (5256113) **4.10** Rugrats. (S) (T) (5858910) **4.35** The Ghost Hunter. (R) (S) (T) (4683910) **5.00** Blue Peter. (S) (T) (5252787) **5.25** Newsround. (S) (T) (3230397)
5.35 Neighbours. (R) (S) (T) (2705719)
6.00 News and Weather. (T) (303)
6.30 Regional News. (755) (**N. Ireland: 6.55 – 7.00** Party Election Broadcast (889026))
7.00 A Question of Sport. With Matt Holland and Alec Stewart. (S) (T) (1262)
7.30 Top of the Pops. (S) (T) (939)
8.00 Eastenders. Alfie gets a warning from Andy. Dennis spies Den and Phil shaking on a deal in the Vic. (S) (T) (6610)
8.30 All About Me. An exhausted Rupinder takes Colin's advice and asks Auntie Jaspreet for help with baby Jay, resulting in a war of words. (S) (T) (2945)
9.00 Absolutely Fabulous. See Pick of the Day. (S) (T) (4571) (**N. Ireland:** Anderson In (4571); **9.30 – 10.00 pm** Absolutely Fabulous (50858))
9.30 Have I Got News for You. (S) (50858)
10.00 News and Weather. (T) (40939)
10.35 Friday Night with Jonathan Ross. With Jerry Springer and *Fame Academy* winner Alex Parks. Plus an exclusive performance by Radiohead. (S) (447216)
11.25 Boxing. Clinton Woods v. Glencoffe Johnson. (568484) (**N. Ireland:** Have I Got News for You (621911); **11.55** Boxing (337736); **1.30** Film: My Very Best Friend (1986, tvm) (84156); **3.00 – 5.30** BBC News 24 (8586886)
1.00 Later with Jools Holland. With Sean Paul, the Coral and Elbow. (S) (T) (107991)
2.55 News. (92742595)
3.35 Mixmasters. (S) (20852798)
4.05 Entertainment Now. (T) (63134601)
4.35 World Football. (S) (T) (63727392)
5.00 Nightscreen. (86682)
5.30 – 6.00 am News. (31458)

3 *Boxing* and *World Football* are ______________________.

4 *What the Romans Did for Us* and *Fast and Dangerous* are ______________________.

5 *News and Weather* and *Regional News* are ______________________.

6 *Friday Night with Jonathan Ross* and *Later with Jools Holland* are ______________________.

THE *-ING* FORM

3 **Use the *-ing* forms of the verbs below to complete this talk about celebrities.**

wear • ~~live~~ • go • do • talk • drive • travel • spend

1 Britney Spears can't imagine *living* a quiet life in the country.

2 Robbie Williams prefers ________________________ his own stunts for his videos.

3 Michael Schumacher likes ________________________ super fast cars.

4 Prince Charles doesn't mind ________________________ to foreign countries.

5 Nicole Kidman loves ________________________ beautiful designer clothes.

6 Rowan Atkinson sometimes can't stop ________________________ in his Mr Bean voice *(Stimme)*.

7 David Beckham enjoys ________________________ time with his wife Victoria and the kids.

8 Queen Elizabeth II enjoys ________________________ for a walk with her Corgis.

-ING FORM OR INFINITIVE?

4 **Reporters asked Gloria Kelly, the young film star of *Frankenstein's Girlfriend*, these questions. Choose the correct verb form.**

1 Can you imagine to work / working as a waitress?

2 Do you prefer to do / doing a love scene with Hugh Grant or Bruce Willis?

3 When did you finish to make / making your last film? And what do you hope to do / doing when this film is finished?

4 Do you want to make / making an action film next?

5 Have you ever tried to give up to smoke / smoking ?

6 When did you learn to dance / dancing ?

PREPOSITION + *-ING* FORM

5 **In these sentences about David Blaine, fill in the preposition *at*, *in* or *of* and the correct form of the verb.**

1 Even as a child, David Blaine was interested ________________________ (do) magic tricks.

2 He was good ________________________ (think) of new stunts to do.

3 He usually isn't afraid ________________________ (injure) himself.

4 David Blaine is good ________________________ (put) together an exciting show.

5 He certainly isn't afraid ________________________ (appear) in public.

6 Blaine is very good ________________________ (use) the media.

7 Are stuntmen interested ________________________ (risk) their lives?

8 His girlfriend is more afraid ________________________ (do) dangerous stunts.

REFLEXIVE PRONOUNS

6 **Gloria Kelly, the film star from *Frankenstein's Girlfriend*, is talking about making the film. Fill in the gaps with the words in the box.**

myself • yourself • herself • himself • itself • ourselves • yourselves • themselves

1 I think the people who see the film will really enjoy ______________________ .

2 In that scene, Bruce Willis started laughing and couldn't stop ______________________ .

3 Most people don't know it, but I always do my stunts ______________________ .

4 One day the makeup artist was ill so we all had to put on our makeup ______________________ .

5 The woman who played my mother tried to write some new lines ______________________ .

6 For that scene, we used a robot which could turn ______________________ around.

7 The director said, "Gloria, you really should teach ______________________ how to shoot a gun."

8 That was a long interview. Now all of you reporters can help ______________________ to some champagne.

EVERYDAY ENGLISH: INSTRUCTIONS

7 **In these instructions, (circle) the letter of the one word that doesn't fit.**

1 Insert your … into the telephone.

a telephone card

b 50 cents

c credit card

(d) computer

2 We have to replace the … in that old car.

a battery

b sofa

c lights

d wiring

3 Next you slide … backwards.

a the cover

b the SIM card holder

c the mechanic

d the battery

4 Remove … from the coffee maker.

a the water

b the coffee

c the coffee pot

d the fridge freezer

5 Close …

a the door

b the back cover

c your book

d the wall

6 Lift up …

a the SIM card holder

b the shop

c the battery

d the chair

8 EVERYDAY ENGLISH: UNDERSTANDING INSTRUCTIONS

Match the instructions for a locker (*Schließfach*) to the pictures.

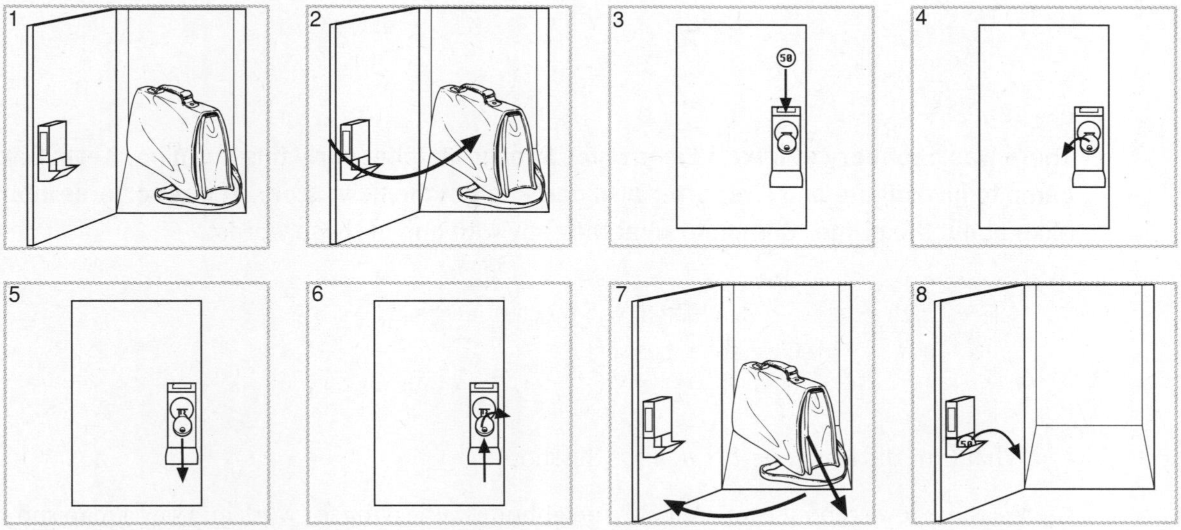

- **a** Remove your 50 cents. ☐
- **b** Turn the key to the left. ☐
- **c** Put your things in the locker. ☐
- **d** Insert 50 cents in the front of the door. ☐
- **e** Open the door and remove your things. ☐
- **f** Close the door of the locker. ☐
- **g** Insert the key and turn it to the right. ☐
- **h** Remove the key. ☐

9 PEOPLE AT WORK: DANGEROUS ACTIVITIES

Which activity is usually dangerous, which is usually safe? Make sentences using the phrases in the box.

▶ **EXAMPLE** *Spending 7 days in a hotel room is usually safe.*
Spending 7 days at the bottom of a big water tank is usually dangerous.

Cleaning windows Smoking 2 cigarettes Climbing Looking at a tiger	in the zoo Mt Everest on the 22nd floor a year an hour in the jungle a 20-metre hill on the ground floor	is usually safe. is usually dangerous.

Cleaning windows ______________________ is usually safe.

Cleaning windows ______________________ is usually dangerous.

Smoking 2 cigarettes ______________________ is usually safe.

Smoking 2 cigarettes ______________________ is usually dangerous.

Climbing ______________________ is usually safe.

Climbing ______________________ is usually dangerous.

Looking at a tiger ______________________ is usually safe.

Looking at a tiger ______________________ is usually dangerous.

UNIT 13 **Fight crime!**

VOCABULARY: CRIME

1 **There was a robbery at *Mike's Electronics Shop* in Datchet early this morning. Kevin Baxter came to investigate and a reporter also came to get the news story. The reporter is interviewing Mike about the crime. Complete what they say with one of these words:**

call • catch • steal • committed • ~~break into~~ • chased • fight • arrest • discovered • punish

R What time did someone *break into*[1] the shop?

M We think it was about 6 am. At 6.30 a neighbour was leaving for work and saw a man run out of the shop with some things. He called to the man, and when he started to run, the neighbour ________________[2] him for a few minutes but he couldn't ________________[3] him.

R Why didn't he ________________[4] the police?

M Well, that's what he did next. Then he called me at home. I went to the shop immediately. The police arrived a few minutes later.

R What did you find?

M I ________________[5] that some mobile phones and cameras were missing. We take away most of them at night, but there were some out on a table.

R Did the robber ________________[6] any money?

M About 100 pounds from the safe. We never lock it at night, and there was only that much in it.

R Did the police find the robber?

M Oh yes, they worked really hard all morning, and around noon they found a suspect with a criminal record. You know somebody ________________[7] two crimes like this in the same area last month. Maybe that was the same man.

R Did they ________________[8] the criminal?

M Of course they did, because when they caught him they even found the mobile phones and cameras in his flat. I hope they ________________[9] him for what he did. We really have to ________________[10] crime in this town.

PASSIVE

2 **Police officer Kevin Baxter is telling his boss what he knows about the crime from exercise 1. Fill the correct form of *be* (1 x present, 8 x past) , then write the past participle of the verb.**

EXAMPLE Mike's Electronics at 223 Elm Street *was broken into* at about 6 am. (break into)

1 A man ______________________ leaving the store with some bags at about 6.30. (see)

2 The shop owner *(Besitzer)* and the police ______________________ at about 6.45. (call)

3 5 mobile phones and 4 cameras ______________________ . (steal)

4 About 100 pounds ______________________ from a safe. (take)

5 The safe ______________ never ______________________ at night. (lock)

6 Five suspects ______________________ in the next 4 hours after the crime. (investigate)

7 A suspect ______________________ in his flat at 247 E. Birch Street with the stolen things. (find)

8 The suspect, John Davis, age 23, __________________ at 12.30 pm and __________________ to prison. (arrest) (take)

PASSIVE – PRESENT PERFECT

3 **Someone broke into this office last night. The secretary calls her boss who is out of town on a business trip. Look at the pictures and complete her sentences with the passive in the present perfect of one of the verbs in the box.**

leave • pull • break into • break • turn over • tidy up • open • steal

EXAMPLE A mess *has been made* in the room.

1 The window ____________________________________ .

2 The cupboards and the desks ____________________________________ .

3 The tables ____________________________________ .

4 The computers ____________________________________ .

5 The telephones ____________________________________ out of the wall.

6 The safe ____________________________________ .

7 A gun ____________________________________ in the room.

8 The room ____________________________________ because the police haven't investigated yet.

PASSIVE

4 **Martin Clarke, Kevin Baxter and Lee's school have helped Lee Dobson to apply for a 3-week vocational school exchange *(Schüleraustausch)* in Germany. Match the parts to complete the sentences.**

Before the trip,

1 a school in Germany ☐
2 many letters and emails ☐
3 the programme for the exchange ☐
4 the necessary application forms ☐
5 rooms for the exchange students ☐
6 travel plans ☐

a were found with local families.
b were written by the two schools.
c were filled in.
d was chosen for the exchange.
e was planned by the teachers.
f were made by the teachers.

During the exchange programme in Germany,

1 plans were made for the German students ☐
2 friends ☐
3 much about work and school ☐
4 mostly English was spoken ☐
5 a wonderful experience and lots of fun ☐
6 part of the money for the programme ☐

a in another European country was learned.
b to come to the UK for 3 weeks.
c was paid by the EU.
d were had by all of the people on the exchange.
e were made.
f by both British and German students.

PASSIVE WITH *BY*

5 **You have learned about all of these people at work. Complete each sentence with *by* and the correct job.**

a plumber • a nurse • a police officer • a mechanic • a youth worker • a shop assistant • an electrician • a caterer

▶ **EXAMPLE** Tricks and stunts are done *by a magician*.

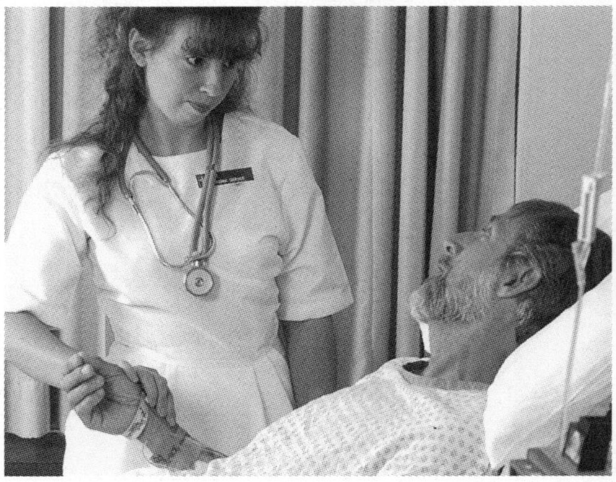

1 A patient's temperature and pulse are checked ______________________.

2 Advice to young people with problems is given ______________________.

3 Cars and machines are repaired ______________________.

4 Customers in a department store are helped ______________________.

5 Wiring is installed and repaired ______________________.

6 A toilet is installed ______________________.

7 Meals are cooked for the people at the recording studio ______________________.

8 Criminals are chased and arrested ______________________.

6 EVERYDAY ENGLISH / PEOPLE AT WORK: INTERPRETING

Here are some things a police officer could say. Interpret them for someone who doesn't speak German.

1 Bitte blasen Sie in diese Tüte.

____, please.

2 Könnte ich bitte Ihren Führerschein sehen?

Could I ____, please?

3 Sie sind 70 gefahren. Hier sind höchstens 55 erlaubt.

___________________________ doing 70. 55 is _________________________________ on this road.

4 Könnten Sie bitte den Räuber für mich beschreiben?

Can you ____?

5 Wie groß war der Räuber?

How ____?

6 Was hatte der Räuber an?

What was ____?

7 Hatte der Räuber ein Schusswaffe bei sich?

Was ____ a gun?

8 Wo waren Sie gestern Abend um 8 Uhr?

____ yesterday evening?

7 EVERYDAY ENGLISH / PEOPLE AT WORK: DESCRIBING PEOPLE

Match the picture of the criminal to the description.

a **b** **c** **d** **e** **f**

1 He is young, between 20 and 30. He is tall and had long blonde hair. He is wearing a sweatshirt and jeans. ☐
2 She is about 40. She had short dark hair and is wearing glasses. She is short and fat. ☐
3 He is quite old, about 70 or 80. He is thin. He is wearing a white shirt and dark suit. ☐
4 She is young, about 15. She is quite slim, but not very tall. She is wearing a T-shirt and short skirt. ☐
5 She is about 40. She had long blonde hair and is quite slim. She is wearing a dress and sunglasses. She is carrying a dog. ☐

Now you write the description of the 6th person.

____

UNIT 14 Boy meets girl

1 THE FIRST DATE

It's Helen's and James's first date. Helen is on her way by bus, and James is waiting for her in the cafe. Here is what they are thinking. Which thoughts go together? Match 1–8 with a–h.

1 Where shall we go later? ☐
2 I was stupid to choose this cafe. ☐
3 I'm going to be late. ☐
4 I can't wear this old jacket again. ☐
5 Have I got enough money? ☐
6 I must check my mobile. ☐
7 Why didn't I ask her out a long time ago? ☐
8 I was stupid to take the bus and not my moped. ☐

a Perhaps James won't wait for me.
b I really need to buy some cool clothes.
c It would be terrible if I had to ask Helen to pay for us both.
d There's a good film on at the Odeon Cinema. Maybe we could go there.
e Maybe there's a message from James.
f This traffic is terrible.
g She's the nicest girl I've ever met.
h It's too expensive and the food isn't very good.

2 PAST PERFECT

After her first date with James, Helen writes an email to her best friend, Sally. For all of the things that happened on the date itself she uses the past tense. For all of the things before the date she uses the past perfect. Fill in the past or past perfect of the verb in her email.

Hi Sally!

I ________________ [1] (have) a fantastic date last night with a guy named James. We ________________ [2] (go) to that cool new cafe near the Odeon cinema and then we ________________ [3] (go) to a film afterwards. I ________________ [4] (meet) James at a dance a few weeks before. Until a few days before our date, he ________________ [5] (have) another girlfriend, but of course they ________________ [6] (break up) before he asked me out. I was actually half an hour late for our date because I ________________ [7] (take) the bus and traffic was awful. But when I ________________ [8] (arrive) at the cafe there was James waiting for me. After the cinema he ________________ [9] (ask) me to go to a party on Friday. That's tomorrow! I can't wait.

Talk to you later, Helen

3

PAST PERFECT – SIMPLE PAST – PRESENT TENSE

After a few months and many, many dates, Helen and James moved into a flat (*Wohnung*) together yesterday. Look at the sentences and sort them into the right category. Look carefully at the tense of the verb to help you decide.

1 James had found a better job as a driver.
2 They carried a lot of things and worked really hard.
3 James is painting the bathroom.
4 They had asked two friends to help them move.
5 They invited Dave and Sally to a restaurant for dinner.
6 Helen and James had bought a fridge and a sofa from a friend.
7 They're finding a place for everything.
8 They're setting up the stereo and TV.
9 They used their friend's car to take all of their things to the new flat.
10 They had looked at about 20 flats.
11 Helen is building new cupboards in the kitchen.
12 They took 20 boxes and their furniture over to the new flat.

Before they moved into the new flat: [1] [ ] [ ] [ ]

Yesterday, the day they moved into the flat: [2] [ ] [ ] [ ]

Now, in the new flat: [3] [ ] [ ] [ ]

4

IF SENTENCES TYPE 3

At dinner in the restaurant, James and Helen are talking with Dave and Sally about how they met. Dave and Sally also talk about how they met. They all think a lot about what would(n't) have happened if… . Life could have been very different. Match the sentence parts.

JAMES AND HELEN

1 If we hadn't gone to the dance that evening, [ ]
2 If Helen had been more than an hour late, [ ]
3 If James's flat had been bigger, [ ]
4 If I hadn't met Helen, [ ]

a we would have stayed there.
b I wouldn't be so happy now.
c we wouldn't have met.
d I wouldn't have waited for her.

DAVE AND SALLY

1 If we hadn't taken summer jobs at that store, [ ]
2 If my family hadn't liked Dave so much, [ ]
3 If we had had enough money, [ ]
4 If I had met Sally 3 years earlier, [ ]

a they wouldn't have invited him for dinner so often.
b we wouldn't have met.
c I wouldn't have stayed with that awful girlfriend so long.
d we would have bought a flat last month.

IF SENTENCES TYPE 3

5 **The daughter of the couple whose story you learned about in Exercise 13 in your course book is now 16 years old and is telling a friend the story of how her parents met 18 years ago. Complete what she says with *had(n't)* + verb or *would(n't) have* + verb.**

▶ EXAMPLE If my father *hadn't been* (not / be) at home, he *wouldn't have answered* (not / answer) the phone.

1 If my mother ____________ (not / be) so bored that evening, she ____________ ____________ (not / try) to call her friend Anita.

2 If she ____________ (not / dial) that wrong number, she ____________ (not / know) about my Dad.

3 If her telephone ____________ (not / have) a re-dial button, she ____________ ____________ (not / call) him back.

4 I think if my Dad ____________ (not / like) her voice too, he ____________ ____________ (not / ask) her out to a cafe.

5 Of course, if they ____________ (not / like) each other on that first date, they ____________ ____________ (not / meet)again.

6 I think they ____________ (not / have) that first date if they ____________ (have) partners and ____________ (be) happy with them.

7 Just think! If my parents ____________ (not / meet), I ____________ (not / be) born.

8 Oh dear, and if I ____________ (not / tell) you this long story, my coffee ____________ ____________ (not / get) cold.

IF SENTENCES TYPE 3

6 **This is the story of how Hans met his partner on a trip to Malta. Put the two thoughts together to show what would / wouldn't have happened if....**

▶ EXAMPLE I went to Malta. I met my wife there.
If I hadn't gone to Malta, I wouldn't have met my wife.

1 I didn't speak English very well. I went to Malta for an English course.

____

____

2 In Malta my passport was stolen. I went to the police station.

____

3 The police officers weren't very fast. I had to wait an hour for them.

____

____

4 Maria's bag was stolen. She went to the police station and waited for the police too.

____

____

5 We didn't have anything else to do. We talked to each other.

____

____

6 Maria didn't have a hotel room yet. I told her about my hotel and she went there.

____

____

7 Every morning we had breakfast together in the hotel dining room. We started to like each other a lot.

____

____

8 Maria didn't speak English very well. I didn't learn a lot of English that week.

____

PEOPLE AT WORK: WORKING WITH A PUBLISHER

7 How is a magazine or a book like this put together? Fill the gaps with the words from the box.

printer • designer and technical staff • editor • journalist • picture researcher • repro studio specialist

The ______________ checks the text.

The ______________ writes the articles.

The ______________ create the finished page.

The ______________ gets the illustrations ready to print.

The ______________ uses very big rolls of paper.

The ______________ looks for photos.

Now match the jobs 1–7 to definitions a–g.

1 enlarge a photo ☐
2 research an article ☐
3 retouch photos ☐
4 create a page ☐
5 correct the text ☐
6 commission the illustrations ☐
7 print the text ☐

a find and change the mistakes
b put the final copy on paper
c design the page
d get information for an article
e make a photo bigger
f make the photos look better
g find someone to do the pictures

UNIT 15 # It's your world

1

REVIEW: *IF* SENTENCES TYPE 1

How can you be more eco-friendly? Match the two halves of these *if* sentences type 1.

1 If I'm fit and it isn't far, ☐
2 If I have an empty deposit can or bottle, ☐
3 If I don't need the lights, ☐
4 If I've got some old batteries, ☐

a I'll walk or cycle.
b I'll put them in the special container at the electro-shop.
c I'll turn them off.
d I'll take them back to the shop.

2

REVIEW: *IF* SENTENCES TYPE 2

Anita dreams of how the environment would be better if she or others had the chance. Fill in the correct form of the verb.

EXAMPLE If I *had* (have) a shop, I*'d / would sell* (sell) only non-returnable bottles.

1 If I ________________ (live) in a warmer country, I ________________________________ (never / use) heating in my flat.

2 If we ________________ (not/have) such good eco-products at Green Garden, I ________________ (get) eco-products from a farmer.

3 If Chris ________________ (try) harder to be more eco-friendly, it ________________ (be) better for our company.

4 If people ______________________ (always / go) to work by car, the traffic problem ________________ (not / be) so terrible.

3

REVIEW: SIMPLE PRESENT AND PRESENT CONTINUOUS

Do you remember these people who you met in your course book? They are all out of their normal routines today. Fill in the correct verb form, present simple or present continuous.

1 Joey usually ________________ the Simpsons on TV at 6 pm, but this evening he ________________ the Winter Olympics. (watch)

2 Sharon and Greg often ________________ by email, but this week Greg is in London so they ________________ in Sharon's favourite cafe. (chat)

3 Veronica, a shop assistant in the clothes department of a store, sometimes ________________ in other departments. This week she ________________ in the cosmetics department. (work)

4 Amy Watson and Rory Hood often ________________ to a country far away for their holiday, but this summer they haven't got so much money so they ________________ in the south of England. (travel)

4 REVIEW: SIMPLE PAST AND PRESENT PERFECT

You are asking questions to some of the other people from this book about their experience. Complete the questions in simple past or present perfect.

TO TERENCE STEWART, WINDOW CLEANER

________________________ the windows of a building in Berlin? (ever / clean)

How many windows ________________________ yesterday? (wash)

How many years ________________________ a window cleaner? (be)

TO HOLLY HENSON, HOLLY'S HELPLINE

________________________ any of the kids who wrote to you? (ever / meet)

________________________ arguments with your parents when you were a teenager? (have)

How long ________________________ your helpline? (have)

"Did you have arguments with your parents when you were a teenager?"

TO DONALD BARBER, HANDYMAN

When ________________________ vocational school? (finish)

What ________________________ last week? (repair)

________________________ a jacuzzi? (ever / install)

Now ask a question to each of the four characters on p 38 of your student's book and write them in your exercise book.

5 REVIEW: SIMPLE PAST AND PAST CONTINUOUS

Anita usually rides her bicycle to work, Chris usually goes by motorbike. Yesterday something unusual happened. Fill in the simple past or the past continuous in this story about Chris and Anita.

Chris ________________ [1] (ride) his motorbike to work yesterday when he suddenly ________________ [2] (see) Anita. She ________________ [3] (sit) next to her bicycle on the side of the road. He immediately ________________ [4] (go) over to her.

"Are you all right?" he asked. "Not really. I've had a little accident. But I think I'm OK." said Anita.

"Oh no, how ________________ [5] (it / happen)?" asked Chris.

Anita looked at him tiredly. "I ________________ [6] (drive) down the highway when a cat suddenly ________________ [7] (run) across the road in front of me. I ________________ [8] (turn) quickly so I wouldn't hit it, and my bike turned over! But two kind people ________________ [9] to help me and ________________ [10] to take me to the hospital."

REVIEW: *-ING* FORM OR INFINITIVE

6 **Anita's boss is on a business trip, and asked her to send him an email about her meeting with the German customer at Green Garden. Choose the *-ing* form or the infinitive in her email and circle the correct form.**

We really tried making / to make [1] Herr Meier feel welcome here and I think we were successful. He seems to be very interested in selling / to sell [2] some of our products in Germany. He doesn't mind coming / to come [3] to England for a sales conference three times a year. I think he rather enjoys travelling / to travel [4], especially to England. He wants opening / to open [5] two stores for eco products in Bavaria next summer and hopes starting / to start [6] another three stores the next year. He prefers doing / to do [7] business in Euros. But he likes our products a lot, so I suggest giving / to give [8] him a very good price.

REVIEW: PASSIVE

7 **Green Garden is having a big conference for all of their sales representatives in a few months. Anita is responsible for it and has made a note of all the things that have to be done. She is checking with her colleagues about what has been done up to now. Make sentences in the passive from her notes.**

- *send out invitations* ✔
- *choose speaker*
- *reserve hotel rooms for guests*
- *write the programme*
- *print the programmes*
- *choose a restaurant for Friday*

1 *Have* the invitations *been sent out*?

2 ____________ the speaker ______________________________?

3 ____________the hotel rooms for guests ______________________________?

4 ____________the programme ______________________________?

5 ____________the programmes ______________________________?

6 ____________a restaurant for Friday ______________________________?

8 REVIEW: USEFUL PHRASES

Another German customer, Herr Müller, is visiting Green Garden in England. He needs some help with his English. Interpret his conversation with Anita Kelly.

HERR M Guten Tag. Wie geht es Ihnen, Ms Kelly?

1 ______________________________

ANITA Oh, hello, Mr Müller. Fine, thanks. It's nice to see you again. Did you have a good journey?

2 ______________________________

____

HERR M Ja, danke. Können Sie mir helfen?

3 ______________________________

Ich habe um 11 Uhr einen Termin mit Herrn Sanderson. Wie komme ich dahin?

4 ______________________________

____

ANITA Take the lift to the 3rd floor. It's room 326, opposite the conference room.

5 ______________________________

____

HERR M Vielen Dank. Bis später.

6 ______________________________

9 PEOPLE AT WORK: REVIEW OF TENSES

Billy Freeman is writing a postcard to his sister about his day as a tour guide yesterday. Fill in the correct verb form: present continuous, present simple, past simple, past continuous, present perfect, or past perfect.

Hi Susan!

How are things in Canada? I'm glad I'm in New Zealand where it's summer! I _'ve been here_ [1] (be) here since 15 November. Up to now I __________ [2] (have) three different tour groups. The one I have now is really difficult. Yesterday while we __________ [3] (walk) in the forest, half of them __________ [4] (get) blisters, the other half __________ [5] (have) bad sunburn. Two days ago a man told me his wallet __________ [6] (be stolen). He __________ [7] (be) in a night club the evening before and __________ [8] (not / be) very careful. So we __________ [9] (spend) all morning at the police station. __________ that ever __________ [10] (happen) to you?

Love,
Billy

Revision puzzle – test yourself!

Answer the questions to fill in important words from your book.
What message can you find in the boxes?

1 □□□□□□□
2 □'□□□□□
3 □□□□□□□□
4 □□□□□□□□□□
5 □□□□□
6 □□□□□□
7 □□□□□□□□□□□

1 She lives in Cologne. She's from … .
2 What time is it in Denver? It's nine … .
3 Dirty is the … of clean.
4 You can buy clothes, food, books, furniture and many other things in a … store.
5 If you want to swim, play volleyball or just lie in the sun, go to the … , but don't forget your sunscreen!
6 If you put red and … together you will get the colour orange.
7 This person can install your lights or repair your wiring.

8 □□□□□□ □□□□□
9 □□□□□□□□
10 □□□□□□□□□

8 Which floor is between the first floor and the third floor?
9 The person who gives you a job is your … .
10 Quick! Call the police and an ambulance. It's an … !

11 □□□□□
12 □□□□□□□
13 □□□

11 How do you close a business letter? … sincerely and then your name.
12 What do you think? What's your … ?
13 Teenagers, like everybody else, have their … and downs.

14 □□□□
15 □□□□□□□□□□□
16 □□□□
17 □□□□□□□
18 □□□□ □□□□

14 I left my money at home. Could you possibly … me 20 euros?
15 I'd like to make an … to see Dr Smith next Tuesday after 4 pm.
16 Your room is a mess! Please … it up immediately.
17 I really … the film. It was really good.
18 You'll find a lot of traffic in any big city during the … … between four and six o'clock, when people go home from work.